SO YOU THINK YOU'RE A CYCLIST?

DOG 'n' BONE

Pete Jorgensen

with illustrations by Paul Parker

SO YOU THINK YOU'RE A CYCLIST?

Cautionary case studies from the city streets

Published in 2014 by Dog 'n' Bone Books
An imprint of Ryland Peters & Small Ltd

20–21 Jockey's Fields   519 Broadway, 5th Floor
London WC1R 4BW   New York, NY 10012

www.rylandpeters.com

10 9 8 7 6 5 4 3 2 1

Text © Pete Jorgensen 2014
Design and illustration © Dog 'n' Bone Books 2014

A CIP catalog record for this book is available from
the Library of Congress and the British Library.

ISBN: 978 1 909313 26 2

Editor: Caroline West
Illustration: Paul Parker
Design: Wide Open Studios

For digital editions, visit
www.cicobooks.com/apps.php

Printed in China

Introduction 6

The Cyclists

INTRODUCTION

There's no getting away from it: bikes are becoming an increasingly important part of our lives. Whether you love or loath them, there are more cyclists on our roads than ever before. It's hard to open a newspaper or turn on the news without being presented with features on new government policies for cycling infrastructure, the successes of pro cyclists at the latest Olympics, or the failures of pro riders at the latest drug test.

Across the cycling world, there are many different motivations for throwing a leg over a top tube and heading out for a ride—some like the fun of going for a spin on a sunny day, while others take it just a tad too seriously. Some people see bikes as the quickest, easiest way to get from A to B; to others, they are potentially the solution to all of the world's environmental problems.

Bikes mean a lot of things to a lot of different people, and the bike world is full of eclectic characters. *So Your Think You're a Cyclist?* aims to identify some of the figures you may meet in the cycling world—like the grumpy bike shop owner who treats you like something he's just scraped off his bottom bracket or the historian who can name every great rider from every grand tour from 1903 to 2003—plus point out some of the quirks and foibles that make them tick.

From a personal perspective, I have been—and still am—many of the characters profiled over the following pages. In my teens, I used to throw myself and my mountain bike down a collection of increasingly steep slopes, hoping I'd come out the other side unscathed. When I started riding again in my mid-twenties, it was on my Dad's battered bike that had been unused for about 15 years and weighed a tonne. I was quickly hooked and became insufferable, as I tried to convince everyone I knew that they too should ride a bike. Within months I was spending hours in front of the TV watching bike races and a small fortune on cycle-related follies— the fixie I built, but never rode, still sits in the hallway, driving my wife insane, as does the stack of cycling-related books piled up in the bedroom. I hope other readers and riders will be able to spot something of themselves or their friends and family in the profiles, too.

BORN-AGAIN CYCLIST

So, you've decided you're going to take up cycling again, but there's a problem—you don't have a bike. Then, you remember your old mountain bike, the one you used to ride to school on. The last time you saw it, it was at the back of the garage at your parents' house; it must still be there. But, a two-hour drive and another two hours spent rummaging through the bombsite your Dad calls a garage has proved to be a complete waste of time.

Undeterred, you visit a local bike shop and are instantly horrified at the prices. You trawl eBay, but struggle to get your head around all the talk of chainsets, hubs, and cranks. You're close to giving up when a friend says that her brother has an old bike he wants to get rid of; it's yours, if you want it.

Next day, you head over to check out the bike. The brother is 5ft 6in, you're 6ft 3in; he's had the bike since he was 14 and, guess what, it still fits him! You give the bike a try and find your knees pressed against your chest, making you look like a cycling fetus, but you're not fussed. The early Nineties' neon paint job is chipped and rust patches pepper the frame, but it's no big deal. The brake pads are completely worn and the cables are loose, but you're okay with that (you'll regret this in around three weeks' time when you ride down your first big hill, can't stop in time, and end up in a bush). You thank the brother for his generosity and take the bike out for your first ride.

You wobble slightly at first, but, as they say, it's just like riding a bike and soon you're getting your confidence up. You start to pick up speed, feel the wind in your hair, and enjoy the freedom cycling gives as you weave through a line of cars stuck in a traffic jam. And then it hits you; you're enveloped by a cloak of complacency, a cocoon of self-satisfaction. You think how much money you'll save on transport, how you're doing your bit for the environment, how much fitter you'll be, how you're contributing to a better world for your children. You feel sorry for the poor saps stuck in their cars, because they don't know the joys that two wheels can bring.

Congratulations, you are now a smug cyclist and, much like ex-smokers, newly weds, born-again Christians, and first-time parents, you're going to bore the hell out of everyone you meet by extolling the virtues of this new existence and how you could never go back to your old ways.

CIVILIZED CYCLIST

In some parts of the world, cycling really isn't a big deal. The fact that a celebrity or a politician is seen riding a bike wouldn't make the front page of a gossip magazine or newspaper. In fact, it wouldn't be news at all, because cycling is simply regarded as a hassle-free way to get from A to B, not the solution to all that's wrong with the world. So, while the citizens of some of the world's greatest cities—London, New York, Paris, and Sydney—are whipping themselves up into a frenzy over a one percent increase in the number of journeys made by bike in the last 10 years, people in Amsterdam, Copenhagen, Seville, and other cycle-friendly towns are shrugging their shoulders and wondering what all the fuss is about.

If you're lucky enough to reside in one of these utopian dream worlds, consider yourself one of the privileged few and stop reading now. If you're one of the rest of us poor saps, living in awe and jealousy of a lifestyle our European cousins take for granted, the following seven entries give a quick summary of some of the differences between us and them.

1. Location:

Us: In an overcrowded city, often in the middle of four lanes of traffic, trying to assert the fact you have as much right to be there as the cars and trucks around you. Easier said than done—this is the two-wheeled equivalent of pissing in the wind.

Them: In a city where the powers that be had the foresight to plan ahead when it came to making decisions on transport infrastructure, rather than desperately scrabbling around promoting highly visible but, ultimately, futile cycling initiatives that offer few long-term benefits to the average rider.

2. Years spent cycling:

Us: Varies wildly. There are some who've been doing it for years but, for many, it's a fairly new activity, often started to save money on ever-increasing transport costs or as a way to lose a few pounds after years of battering bodies with a cocktail of fried food, booze, and general inactivity.

Them: First came walking, soon after came cycling; the two have been almost interchangeable ever since. And it's something that will continue well into middle age, as almost every household will have regular access to a bike or two.

3. Bike choice:

Us: For him, the best bike he can afford and often highly unsuitable for the task at hand. It will usually be purchased after days spent on the Internet researching brands or establishing what's cool in the bike world. For her, the sporty type will go for a hybrid or a racer, while those not so exercise-inclined will be tempted by something that looks old-fashioned and comes with a basket.

Them: Nothing ostentatious; almost always a sit-up-and-beg bike, often with a luggage rack or basket, plus mud guards to stop you getting a soaked backside when riding in the rain. For many, practicality rather than performance is the key.

4. Outfit:

Us: A collection of outfits, usually made from synthetic materials and often costing obscene amounts, which are designed specifically for cycling or other sporting activities. A helmet is worn by the paranoid and largely ignored by those who don't like to be told what to do, feel stupid having a cranium that resembles a mushroom encased in plastic, or are particularly worried about messing up their hair.

Them: Whatever they plan to wear for the other activities they are going to do that day. No special clothing is required.

5. Terrain:

Us: Take what you can get, whether it be roads pock-marked with holes, cycle paths that stop almost as soon as they've started, multi-lane junctions shared with trucks, or narrow lanes with barely enough room for a bike to pass, let alone a car.

Them: A well-connected, comprehensive network of bike lanes that offers users a quick and safe passage through the city and out into the countryside.

6. Amount of time spent talking about cycling:

Us: A lot. Whether it's discussing equipment, bragging about the length of a recent ride, sharing a thrilling tale about a recent puncture, or trying to convince non-cycling friends that they should give it a go, the amount of airtime given to bike-based chatter soon adds up.

Them: It's a bit like asking how many hours you spend talking about breathing. It's not seen as a big deal, so you just don't talk about it.

7. Enemies:

Us: Everyone's against you: cars, pedestrians, the government, the kid at the end of the road who shouts "fat bastard" as you ride past in your bib shorts. It's like a war zone out there.

Them: Mechanical failure, the odd puncture, or an unexpected rain shower. Otherwise, the overall atmosphere is pretty congenial.

First Time In Clips Rider

For many, cycling can be a slippery slope. What started off innocently as a way to get from A to B can quickly take over your life and your wallet. You find yourself struggling to fight the desire to purchase more and more kit to improve your cycling experience, whether this is carbon fiber brake levers to make your bike marginally lighter or insulated water bottles that keep the liquid inside cooler for at least an extra three minutes. Worth every penny.

One of the first upgrades many cyclists make is to clipless pedals, or cleats, a system designed to lock a rider's feet to the pedals, without the need for cumbersome straps and toe clips. The benefit of being fixed to your bike is that it supposedly makes pedaling up to 25 percent more efficient and can help you cycle up hills more easily. Whether you'll notice this on the three-mile jaunt to the office, through heavy rush-hour traffic, remains up for debate. Still, that doesn't put most people off and, as well as purchasing the pedals, they also go out and buy special shoes that look like props created by an LSD-addled costume designer for a Sixties' sci-fi movie. Make no mistake, the shoes that enable you to use cleats are some of the most horrendous fashion creations known to man. And yet, riders choose to spend extortionate amounts on shoes that wouldn't even have been considered acceptable in the Eighties, a decade notorious for its countless crimes against fashion and good taste.

The real joy of the clipless pedal, however, comes to anyone lucky enough to see a cyclist attempt a first outing with feet firmly bolted to the bike. Echoing the film scene in which Bambi takes his first steps on the ice, the rider will start by tentatively trying to clip in and out of the cleats, while leaning against a wall for support. After a few successful attempts, confidence levels grow and he'll try a few laps around the local park, reassured by the soft landing offered by the grass should he fail to clip out safely.

Once the fear of falling off has been conquered and clipping in becomes second nature, the intrepid adventurer heads for the road. It's now that the rest of us are in for a treat. The rider approaches a set of traffic lights, forgets his feet are firmly fixed to the bike, and falls helplessly into the road, much to the hilarity of all motorists, pedestrians, and fellow riders in the vicinity. The rider then flails around on the floor like an upturned tortoise, desperately trying to release himself from the mechanical clutches of his bindings, until he eventually manages to kick free. Bright red and mortified by a very public mishap, the failed clip user quickly dusts himself off before remounting the bike and cycling away as fast as possible, looking only at the floor and never at the laughing crowd behind. The other clip-using riders smile, as they remember their first time in cleats, too. It's a right of passage for any cyclist to fall ass-over-tit soon after investing in a set.

MAMIL

In order to truly understand the behavior of the MAMIL, or Middle-Aged Man In Lycra, one has to observe him in his natural habitat: the road. It is here that he will spend many hours, often leaving behind the female and his young as he embarks on expeditions to new territories, sometimes covering in excess of 60 miles a day.

The evolution of the MAMIL is fascinating. At around the age of 40, he suddenly develops a deep fascination with two wheels, tight clothing, and expensive accessories. Scientists are divided as to the cause of this obsession, with some hypotheses claiming the cause to be a MAMIL's realization of his own mortality. Others state a desire to become more attractive to potential mates as the key factor, while some schools of revisionist anthropology suggest a need to bond with other MAMILs is the catalyst for trussing up his not-insubstantial body mass in ill-fitting outfits. Whatever the motivating factors, the desire to spend a small fortune on equipment is one that most MAMILs are unable to resist.

MAMILs can often be spotted traveling in packs. They venture out into the wild on a weekly basis and, on a Sunday morning, one will often find roads teeming with MAMILs eager to socialize. These groups are usually easy to spot and each member will have a sleek exterior and bulbous upper skull. The external skeleton of an emerging MAMIL can often be gelatinous and blubbery, much like that of a seal preparing for a cold winter in the Atlantic, but, by the end of a period of regular activity, he will hope to have shed this weight in favor of a more lithe appearance. The markings on a MAMIL vary greatly but are often distinctive—they will be covered in a variety of bold colors and decorated with scripts used to appeal to other MAMILs. Some remain obsessed by their appearance, often preening and posing in an attempt to fit in with other members of the group. These popinjays periodically shed their skin to reveal new markings designed to impress. It is a sad quirk of nature that such efforts are usually met with mirth and derision from both their mates and their offspring.

Typically, the velocity of MAMILs varies greatly, with average speeds generally inversely proportionate to the size of the specimen. The larger MAMILs tend to have lived a previously sedentary existence, which has dictated that they are most comfortable traveling on flat terrain and will actively seek out ways to avoid crossing mountainous areas. When confronted with an incline, a MAMIL's face has a chameleon-like ability to change from its natural color to a bright crimson and he will omit a hissing, puffing sound similar to that of an injured gnu. The smaller MAMILs, more suited to vigorous exercise, will use such opportunities to assert their dominance over the bigger members of the group by upping their speeds on an ascent.

In conclusion, one can accurately say that the global population is in rude health, with numbers on the increase and showing no signs of slowing down any time soon.

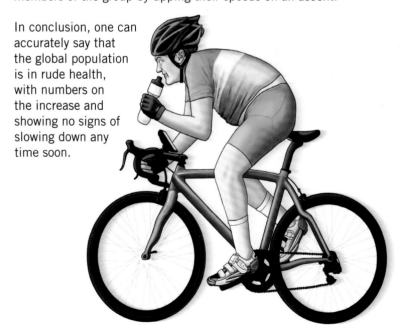

SPORTIVER

On any given weekend during the cycling season, which usually runs from around March to October, thousands of riders across the cycling world will be gearing up to take part in a sportive. To give it its full name, the cyclosportive is an organized event in which riders take part in a timed challenge, usually over relatively long distances, in an attempt to test themselves and their fellow riders. It can also be referred to as a gran fondo, but we'll go with the French version to reward them for the sterling effort they've put in over the years to expand the cycling vernacular.

At the start line, you will find a whole host of characters ready to ride the sportive, each with a different goal. Here are some of the characters to keep an eye out for:

The Rabbit in the Headlights:

Who: The first-time attendee, with little to no experience and questionable fitness.

Reason for riding: His friend was doing it and convinced him it would be a good idea.

Reaction at the finish: Speak to him in a couple of days when he's able to concentrate on something other than the searing pain shooting through his legs, chest, and lower back.

The Old Hand:

Who: A rider with over 200 sportives under the straps of his bib shorts and, hopefully, another 200 more before his legs give up.

Reason for riding: He's not quite sure. This person has been doing sportives for so long, they've just become a habit.

Reaction at the finish: Jadedness—he doesn't even bother to pick up a goodie bag at the end of the race.

The Panicker:

Who: Another first-time rider, but with aspirations. This person wants to do well, so has dedicated hours of training in preparation for the big day.

Reason for riding: He is nervous about taking part in what he sees as a huge undertaking, but feels it's about time he put himself to the test.

Reaction at the finish: What was all the fuss about? He has completed several training rides that were considerably harder than the route he's just finished.

The Nutritionist:

Who: Rider who has carefully planned out her exact dietary requirements, not just for the race, but for the three weeks beforehand as well.

Reason for riding: Health. You can't just eat well; you also have to exercise in order for your body to be in tip-top condition.

Reaction at the finish: Jeez, all those energy gels, grain bars, hydration sachets, and isotonic sports drinks cost me a small fortune. Still, worth every penny.

The Charity Rider:

Who: An exceptionally bubbly, positive character who thinks that it's a good idea to attempt to ride 150 miles up a mountain in searing summer heat, while dressed as a Disney character.

Reason for riding: A kind soul and an altruistic desire to help those in need.

Reaction at the finish: This person retains a cheery disposition, even when faced with a trip to Ikea on a public holiday when there's a sale on, so expect an ebullient mood upon completion of the ride.

The Competitor:

Who: The rider who lives by the motto: second place is the first loser, and has this tattooed on his forearms to inspire him while he rides.

Reason for riding: Are you stupid? To win!

Reaction at the finish: Depending on the result, either vomit-inducing statements of false modesty and sportsmanship or an exceptionally quick exit back home followed by a sulk of epic duration.

The Veteran:

Who: A senior member of the cycling world who's been actively riding for as long as he can remember, which is way before most of us were a twinkle in our parents' eye.

Reason for riding: If he stopped now, there'd be a good chance he'd never start again.

Reaction at the finish: Pass me my oxygen, dear boy, now there's a good chap.

The Pack:

Who: A group of friends or club riders who mean business.
Reason for riding: To live out their Tour de France fantasies by controlling the ride and drafting their way to the finish line.
Reaction at the finish: That bit where we caught the breakaway, then led from the front for the final 15k, it was just like Stage 11 of the '97 Tour. Amazing!

The Complainer:

Who: Experienced sportiver and ray of sunshine who loves to hate the whole experience.
Reason for riding: A desire to tell the organizers exactly what it is they're doing wrong. In his eyes, he provides a public service; to everyone else he's the human equivalent of saddle sore.
Reaction at the finish: The way the ride bunched up at the first climb was ridiculous—have they not heard of staggered starts? And why did the marshals not request that slower riders move to the left to let more experienced cyclists through. A complete waste of a perfectly good Sunday.

The Walker:

Who: Person who likes riding bikes, but just hates the hills.
Reason for riding: To avoid any gradients steeper than 0.5°, unless they're going downhill, of course. If faced with such a challenge, he is straight off his bike and walks his way to the top, and then freewheels his way down with a huge smile on his face.
Reaction at the finish: The downhill stretches were fantastic.

TRACK RIDER

For many, the beauty of cycling is the chance that it provides for riders to enjoy the great outdoors. Pedal enthusiasts talk in reverent tones about the experience of feeling the wind in your hair as you propel yourself happily through some of the finest countryside nature has to offer.

The track cyclist, on the other hand, thinks that's bullshit. Why waste your time cycling up a mountain to enjoy the spectacular view once you've reached the summit when, instead, you could enjoy cycling around and around the same hundred meters of track, day in and day out, as you train for your next race (which, unsurprisingly, means more dizzying laps, just at a slightly different venue). If variety is the spice of life, then track cyclists want nothing to do with it. Who cares about interesting routes, scenic rides, and breathtaking descents when you've got the sterile and precise environment of the velodrome to enjoy?

Other riders may well be excellent at riding up hills, but that matters not one jot to the track star. Here, it's purely about speed and endurance on the flat, and countless hours are spent each week in the quest to cut down personal best times by one-hundredth of a second. Or, in other words, significantly less time than it takes for your TV to respond to the request from your remote control to switch off once you've realized track cycling is the only thing on.

Equipment-wise, the bikes cost many thousands to develop and weigh next to nothing, but then they only have one enormous gear. This is fine if you plan to cycle home from work at an average speed of 40 mph, but less useful if you're just nipping to the shops to pick up some milk for your morning bowl of cornflakes. Try to pedal on a gear that's the size of a dinner plate, and the strain could potentially lead to, at best, muscle damage, at worst, following through.

And then there are the outfits. Dressed up in their super-aerodynamic skin suits, shoes that make them waddle like a duck, and helmets that appear to be modeled on a door-stop, they wouldn't look out of place locked up in the dungeon of a debauched Berlin fetish club. But looking cool is not the focus here; speed is, which is lucky when you consider the aim of one of the events, the keirin, is to chase after a man tootling slowly along on an old-fashioned motorbike... you can almost hear the Benny Hill music as they loop around the track. To buy all this would cost more than the average person's annual salary, which is why most sensible people are happy to shun a life of limitless laps—the cycling equivalent of groundhog day if you wish—and, instead, use their bikes to take pleasure in the chance to explore the outside world, or get that much-needed carton of milk from the store.

COMPETITOR

I started bike racing when I was in my teens. Back then I was quite small in size and so a sport that benefits the lighter frame was ideal for me. I wouldn't say I was particularly competitive, but I absolutely can't stand losing. It puts me in a foul mood for days after a race, but, other than that, I'm pretty laid back about sports.

On average, I usually spend 20 hours a week on the bike. My partner Chris says I take training too seriously, but he doesn't understand that it's just a hobby. It's nothing compared to what the pros put themselves through—they do at least 22.

The week before a race, I'm usually tapering, so won't be out on the bike as much; I just do a few miles after work. I'm usually back home by 10pm, so I get to spend a good bit of quality time with my man. I need to be in bed by 10:45pm to maximize my recovery, but those extra 45 minutes together makes all the difference. As the saying goes: the couples that make time for each other, stay with each other. We sometimes have a romantic meal together, which I love to do. My diet means I'm mainly on poached chicken breasts and plain rice, but I spice this up by adding a dash of sauce—it's a special occasion after all. There have been times when I've even stolen a bite of curry from Chris' plate. The saturated fats and excess salt and sugar mean I have to train for an extra hour in the morning, but you have to treat yourself once in a while.

We usually relax with a few stretches and some deep tissue massage, just like any normal couple. Chris is a whizz with his hands—he always manages to bring even the most tired muscles back to life. After that, we'll probably watch a movie, some TV, or some videos we've shot to analyze my riding position. We used to have a Nintendo console and played a lot of Wii Sports; it was such fun. I was pretty good, but I could never get the hang of the baseball. Once when we were playing, and Chris was winning, I unintentionally let go of the controller as I swung for the ball and it hit Chris square in the face. It was an unfortunate accident, but Chris sold the Wii not long after that.

The morning of a race usually starts with me giving myself an enema. Amateurs think this is pretty gross, but, I can assure you, the pros do it all the time and it's a very clean procedure. Sure, you make a bit of a mess the first few times, but Chris used to clean up after me while I went to prepare my breakfast of quick-release carbs. After a while, the whole procedure becomes second nature and losing those extra few grams makes all the difference, trust me. We always head to the start of the race together, but we have a tradition that we don't meet at the finishing line unless I win. He'll usually ask one of the coaches to text him the result and, if I win, he'll come over and give me a big hug. If I lose, I'll usually make my own way home. We started this routine because Chris said he hated to see me lose; it's just too upsetting for him and he doesn't want me to see him cry. It's nice that he's so concerned for my wellbeing. I'm lucky to have him.

COURIER

Dressed up in torn denim and a battered T-shirt, and looking like he's just come from the audience of a hardcore punk show, the bike courier weaves his way in and out of traffic at high speed. On his back is an oversized messenger bag filled with packages and envelopes sent by the capitalist scum he loves to hate. As he pedals faster and faster, he screams at other riders, drivers, and pedestrians to get out of the way. After all, he's got an important delivery to make, and nobody's going to stand in the way of him getting his package there on time.

Bike couriers like to think of themselves in fairly self-aggrandizing terms: an underground gang of postal pirates operating outside the laws of stamps, mail boxes, and last collection times. They stick a middle finger up at traditional delivery methods, choosing instead to distribute packages on their terms—or at least those of the courier company that hires them—and in the fastest time possible. But, what these puffed-up posties don't realize is that, while in their own eyes they are knights of the road, laws-unto-themselves, and worshipped by office workers across the city as saviors of deadlines, to others, they're just the sweaty, scruffy guys into whose grease-encrusted hands you thrust an overdue invoice.

And, while these mail mercenaries are out all day in all weather conditions, busting their asses delivering parcels for less than the minimum wage, their colleagues at the Post Office are getting decent pay, decent perks, and a decent holiday allowance. When a bike courier gets sick, he doesn't get paid; when he takes a holiday, he doesn't get paid; when he gets knocked off his bike, having tried to squeeze through an impossibly tight gap in order to get the creative department that disc of high-res images that they'll ignore until Tuesday, he doesn't get paid. Still, bike messengers get to wear cut-off denim shorts, faded cycling caps, and wife-beaters whenever they want. Plus, they have a collection of really edgy tattoos, saying things like "fuck cars" or "I hate taxis" and can tell you where all the good coffee shops are around town, so, y'know, it's kind of worth it.

HIPSTER

I used to ride fixed, but, you know, the scene kind of died. When every second person you see is riding the same type of bike, it's a sure sign that it's not cool anymore. I pride myself on originality, so it was time for a change. For me, now, it's all about the custom build. It wasn't anything to do with most of the coolest bike blogs switching their focus from track to road; that was just coincidence. It definitely shouldn't come as a surprise to you that I'm once again ahead of the curve.

My job as a trend forecaster means I'm a taste-maker. I inspire people with my lifestyle, my way of thinking. People want to be me, so, if Joe public sees me looking cool on my road bike, it's only natural that he would want to emulate that. In a way, it's my gift to the world. But, once they cotton on that it's cool, I'll be moving on to the next thing.

For now, at least, my focus is on custom frames. When you're putting your body through a strenuous cycling regime, as I do, you need a frame that fits like a glove. In my day-to-day life I cycle to meetings all over London—Dalston, Hackney, Old Street—I cover at least 3 miles a day. Once, I even went down as far as Peckham for a Fashion Week party. I'm not making that mistake again; I was too tired. Even a couple of lines in the bathroom couldn't perk me up and I had to get a cab back up east. Do you have any idea how hard it is to convince a driver to put a bike in his cab? It didn't even make a difference when I told him that my bike was worth more than his car. Some people.

Anyway, back to the bike. I'm really into my custom lugwork. You probably don't know what that is, but let me put it in the simplest terms: it gives the frame-builder a real chance to show me his individuality, and that's what I'm all about. With regard to graphics, it's tough to choose, but my job as a color forecaster makes it easier. The Pantone Book is like my bible. I'm currently trying to find the exact Pantone for EPO so I can match it to the yellow of Lance's jersey. The bike badge is going to be a needle going through the heart of 6 million cycling fans. LOLZ.

I'm also really into the social side of the custom scene. My friends and I recently set up a cycling club. We haven't really ridden anywhere yet, but my mate has just graduated from Central St. Martins and designed us a sick jersey. We usually just cruise over to *Look Mum No Hands* for an espresso or flat white. It's where cyclists in the know go for their caffeine fix. There are some great places for coffee down in Clerkenwell, but that's where the couriers hang out and we don't see eye to eye. I tried to offer them a bit of friendly advice that bike messengers were in danger of becoming a bit passé, but they wouldn't listen. Well, the joke's on them if they think style bloggers are going to run features on couriers in the next decade.

FIXIE RIDER

Brakes and gears are two of the most essential items on any bike and ones that any sane rider would choose in favor of clipless pedals, carbon seatposts, and the latest Garmin satellite navigation systems. So, how do you explain the phenomenon of the fixie bike, where owners have done away with the components that are key to a) stopping quickly and safely, and b) helping you carry on going when gradients become more tricky? The simple answer: they are simpletons.

The anachronistic use of the fixie on modern roads can be attributed to one group in particular: hipsters. That collective of city-dwelling twenty-somethings determined to stand out from the crowd by dressing exactly like all their friends who have also raided their grandparent's wardrobes for ironic clothing.

Not happy about the functionality of modern bikes, with their restrictive components and corporate

branding, they rebelled by stripping perfectly good bikes of all their useful features—like the ability to stop quickly—and, instead, covered them in stickers, aerospoke wheels, and the ubiquitous brightly colored saddle and bar tape. In fact, serious amounts of money were spent in the quest to make something worse than it originally was. Go figure.

When questioned about why they feel the need to make their lives harder and the experience of cycling more dangerous, fixie riders react with a venom usually only reserved for rapists, paedophiles, Justin Bieber, and baristas who fail to draw a pretty little fern in the foam of their morning latte.

"Riding fixed is riding in its purest form; we don't need bells, whistles, and frills. All we require are two wheels and the road." You'd love to share their passion for the impractical, but the last irrelevant thing you felt that strongly about was the fact that Ricky Gervais never made a third series of *The Office*, so let's leave them to it.

As is often the case with hipster trends, the fixie has now been co-opted by members of the public (and who said that society was being dumbed down?). The result: members of the self-proclaimed urban elite are espousing custom bikes rather than fixies (see page 30). This leaves a new gang in town, riding cheaply made Chinese frames purchased at highly inflated prices from (bizarrely) high-street clothes shops. For the time-being, it's probably the simplest, yet perhaps not the safest, option to allow them to temporarily enjoy their new toys. After a few rides spent wheezing their way up hills and struggling to stop as they make their way down again, it'll only be a matter of time before they trade no gears and no brakes for something a little more practical.

VINTAGE PRINCESS

The vintage life doesn't come easily; you've got to work for it. I'm really not happy about these girls who think they can buy a tea dress from Topshop or Urban Outfitters, and suddenly they're "retro." Urghh, I hate that word! People need to learn one dress does not a vintage-lover make. It takes constant commitment applied to every aspect of your life, from the hair products you use to the plates you eat your dinner from. It even applies to the mode of transport you choose, and that's why I ride a Sixties' Schwinn bicycle.

I picked my bike up for an absolute steal at a garage sale when I went back to visit my parents on the East Coast. I got it for just a few bucks—so much better than what you'd pay for it at a bike store back in Austin. They know people are prepared to pay top dollar for a bike that's as nice as mine, but I'm all about the thrill of the deal. Finding a bargain is one of the best feelings you can imagine—even better than the taste of the cronut I ate while I was interning at a New York fashion magazine last summer! The shipping costs to get the Schwinn back home weren't as cheap as I'd have liked, but it wasn't a problem because Dad offered to pay. Thanks, Daddy... mwah! I was having a craft party with my friends when the UPS guy dropped it off. You should've seen their faces—they were so jealous. Their complexions almost turned the same shade as the mint juleps I'd made everyone using a recipe I found in a 1920s original copy of *Good Housekeeping* magazine! I had a minor setback when I unboxed the bike, in that it didn't actually work—the wheels were buckled and wouldn't move and the brakes seemed not to want to budge—but a quick call to Pop sorted that. He wired me some extra cash and I whizzed down to the local bike store as fast as my brogues would carry me. The man told me I was wasting my money, that the amount it would cost to fix the Schwinn would be so much better spent on a new bike, that newer models weighed considerably less and had more than three gears. He clearly knows absolutely nothing about vintage.

Anyway, now the bike's up and running and it's a real beauty. The first thing I did was tie some dried flowers to the front and decorate it with a few ribbons from my sewing box. Too cute! Then, of course, you've got to get a wicker basket; it makes shopping for groceries at the farmers' market so much easier. I must confess it doesn't handle hills that well, but, as I've said before, you have to make sacrifices to live the vintage lifestyle and, if that means I have to carry a spare tea dress with me, as I'm dripping with sweat, it's still totally worth it.

FEMME FATALE

A vision in purple and white, the Femme Fatale stands out in a sea of lycra and sportswear like a clean rider on Lance Armstrong's cycling team. Dressed as if she's just stepped off the catwalk, the Femme Fatale is a vision of imperturbable elegance as she makes her way to work, completely oblivious to anything that's going on around her and with a total disregard for the rules of the road.

Regular commuters are floored, as they watch a mass of flowing hair run a red light and go straight into the middle of a busy intersection. But somehow she always survives, her radiant beauty acting like a force field to protect her from any oncoming vehicle. Her beauty literally stops traffic.

There's a lot to get worked up about on a bike in the city; it can be quite a stressful experience. You need to have your head on a swivel, ready to react to any unexpected scenarios, such as a friendly taxi driver who cuts you up as he makes a U-turn, the oblivious driver that opens a door just as you're about to pass, or the super-keen rider who wants to engage you in small talk at 7am before you've had a morning coffee. And yet the Femme Fatale doesn't seem to be troubled by the same issues that affect your average rider. Instead, she chooses to maintain a constant zen-like state of absolute serenity whenever she steps on a bike. Nothing seems capable of hurting her as she drifts into oncoming traffic without a care in the world, charges through crossings filled with pedestrians, and turns into side streets with no attempt at signaling her intent to do so. Some riders hate her, others are in awe of her, but one thing is for

Femme Fatale

certain, she couldn't give a shit what you think, even if she did ever notice you.

Her head always remains without a helmet because it plays havoc with her hair. Instead, she wears a wide-brimmed hat and her ears are covered with headphones playing something kitsch from the Fifties to help drown out the car horns and shouts that follow her wherever she rides. The Femme Fatale did once consider riding in flat shoes, but the thought of wearing running shoes repulsed her and it was only something extra to fit in the basket. Instead, she carries on to work as normal, a calming presence in the otherwise frantic world of commuters.

And, when she arrives on her Pashley, she simply smoothes down her dress, smiles sweetly at the receptionist, and glides to her desk, leaving her fellow cycling co-workers to head to the showers to clean off the sweat accumulated on their rides and share stories of this crazy woman they saw who nearly caused an accident as she rode across three lanes of oncoming cars.

13

RED LIGHT RENEGADE

The relationships between cyclists, other road users, and pedestrians might sometimes be best described as challenging, but, for the most part, they coexist in relative harmony. However, if there is one person who can turn a pedestrian crossing the road or a car driver waiting at a junction into a seething ball of fury, it's a Red Light Renegade.

One of the many joys of cycling, particularly for the daily commuters, is the ability to cut calmly through traffic, traveling at a speed considerably higher than the almost stationary line of cars left in their wake. This has a tendency to hack off drivers running late for work who have moved just 100 yards in the last 20 minutes. But, if you really want to see a driver crippled by paroxysms of rage, you need to witness the reaction when a cyclist fails to acknowledge the presence of a red light.

Blissfully unaware that he is the reason for the chorus of expletives resonating from motionless vehicles and the sound of fists thumping angrily on dashboards, the renegade weaves through the traffic. He hears the blast of car horns behind him and thinks to himself, "I pity those poor people, so stressed about all this traffic. Rather than beep their horns in frustration, they should try riding a bike, it's so much quicker."

Next, the renegade approaches a pedestrian crossing. The green man is flashing, indicating safe passage for the crowd waiting patiently at the roadside. As they step out into the street, a woman with a young child and an elderly gentleman soon realize that the rider hurtling toward them has ignored the red light telling him to stop, choosing instead to maintain both his course and his speed. As he narrowly avoids scything down a pair of schoolchildren, a woman, and a dog, the insults fly once again, as screams of "It's green, you bastard!" and "I hate cyclists!" fill the air. One particularly livid man attempts to give chase, but the Red Light Renegade is long gone.

Having arrived at his destination, the rule-averse renegade dismounts after another successful journey and looks at his watch, impressed at his time. "This is why I love cycling," he thinks, completely unaware of the damage he's caused to the reputation of riders across the city.

On his way home, however, his outlook changes. He jumps a red light in front of the same elderly gent he nearly flattened earlier, unaware of a police car behind him. The sirens sound, the renegade stops sheepishly, the man smiles. "Justice," the old boy thinks. Sadly, karma must be taking a break from this corner of town and the car screeches off—the cops obviously have bigger fish to fry. The renegade carries on his way, leaving the old codger struggling to control his rapidly rising blood pressure.

COMMUTER

Across the world, the number of people choosing to ride to work, rather than drive or get public transport, is increasing at a rapid rate. From the residents of Amsterdam, who've been doing it way before anyone else thought to copy them, to the suited-up New York men and women on their way to a meeting and the Londoners who love nothing more than getting fully lycra-ed up to travel the two miles to the office and back.

There are numerous benefits to riding to work, which most commuters will be only too happy to tell you about. Whether it's the fact it helps to wake you up in the morning and prepare you for the day, or that cycling will save you thousands on ticket prices or fuel costs over the course of a year. Admittedly, all these factors are pretty great and hard to ignore, but, if you have no desire to own a bike, they can get pretty tiresome.

Yes, the cost aspect is tempting—nearly everyone could do with a little bit extra in the bank at the end of the month, but surely this is negated by the need to be constantly spending money on your bike. Firstly, there was the cost of buying the thing. You may have managed to dodge this by getting hold of an old bike, but it's more than likely you soon had to take it into a shop to get it repaired. Once your ride is back up and running, things go well for a few weeks or months as confidence grows in direct correlation with smugness levels, but then you are forced to choose a new route to take: Path A or Path B. Those who take Path A will start to feel envious of those who travel faster than them and look for reasons why this is happening. "I wonder if that frame is lighter than mine, or is it because of those clip-in shoes?" they'll ponder, before heading online or to the local bike shop to throw money at the problem. Bike envy is a vicious cycle (pardon the pun), and it continues until you realize you've wasted a fortune on pointless bits and pieces aimed at getting you to the office a few seconds faster.

Those who take Path B are uninterested in speed competition, but will face their own demon: the weather. Most likely a warm, sunny spell helped with the motivation to get on a bike in the first place, but, as winter approaches and temperatures drop, the idea of heading out into the wind, rain, and maybe even snow quickly becomes less appealing than jumping in the car or onto a train. Soon you're back with all the rest of us average commuters, having spent considerably more on your bike than we did on travel costs in the short period you were riding. Oh well, there's always next year.

In conclusion, while we're happy that you are getting out, getting fit, and perhaps saving money in the process, can you please pipe down about it and maintain a sense of perspective? The rest of the commuting world would like to continue our journeys in peace. So, if you could leave us to smile quietly from our seat on the bus, as we watch you trying to change a puncture in the pouring rain, while attempting to avoid getting oil on your work clothes, that would be great.

CITY BIKE HIRER

"Everybody hates a tourist, especially when they think it's such a laugh," sang Pulp frontman Jarvis Cocker. And, although his statement was aimed at rich people pretending to be poor, the same sentiment can apply to those who decide to take advantage of the bike hire schemes popping up in major cities across the globe.

New York, Paris, Barcelona, London, Rio, Melbourne, and Beijing are all in on the act, having set up systems whereby people can hire bikes from docking stations dotted around the city for little to no cost. On paper, the enterprise is a great idea and for many the system works well, offering users an alternative to public transport to get round the city. But when a bike is placed in the hands of an interloping visitor who has no clue where they are, even less idea where they are going, and isn't even too confident that they're traveling on the right side of the road, the situation has got disaster written all over it.

Many tourists, particularly younger ones, are drawn to cycle-hire schemes like backpackers to budget hostels with cut-price drinks offers. The happy-go-lucky riders release the bikes from the docking station in the city-center park and start riding. The novelty of cycling for the first time since they were kids has everyone smiling and posing for photographs, gradually getting increasingly cocky as the wacky racers in the group attempt wheelies and bunny hops. Nothing is guaranteed to piss off a local more than people having fun, particularly when they are trying to enjoy a quiet lunch and their ham sandwich has just been coated in a fine layer of dust caused by an overzealous skid. Soon, the tourists are embracing their inner stuntmen: riding at top speed over humps and bumps, attempting to get some elusive air, and putting bikes onto walls and dropping off them onto the ground. One idiot even decides to ride through a fountain. It's hilarious if you're in your twenties and on holiday. For everyone else it's about as funny as watching back-to-back Ashton Kutcher comedies.

Soon, all opportunities for park-based high jinx are expended and the happy pack go off in search of new adventures. They head out of the gates, but the smiles are soon wiped from their faces as they emerge from the peaceful setting of the park and into three lanes of fast-moving traffic. The local motorists give them a friendly welcome. "Get out the bloody road," "Move over you c***," and "Watch where you're going," ring in the tourists' ears when they miss a turning and get sucked into a one-way system. As they pedal tearfully down an underpass, they realize that they are trapped like rats beneath the city, surrounded by gas-guzzling predators rushing past them at high speed. They grit their teeth, pray, and pedal furiously until they exit out of the other side of the tunnel. Luckily, the lights change and the traffic draws to a halt, allowing the frightened tourists to head for safety and check for potentially sullied undergarments. "That's it," they say, "Never again, we'll stick to the subway." And they mean it, until the next evening when, after a night at a particularly raucous tourist trap, they decide to play with fire once again.

COPENHAGEN OBSESSIVE

Up until a few years ago, if you'd asked someone to tell you something about Denmark, they'd either talk about Lego bricks and bacon or how much they love Dutch people and the fact weed is legal in Amsterdam... So, it came as some surprise to the Danes that in recent years their country, and in particular the capital, Copenhagen, has become the focal point for smug people across the world.

The foodies crowed how foraging and New Nordic Cuisine were the most thrilling developments in cooking since the last pointless thing they were excited about. The culture vultures proclaimed Danish television dramas to be must-see shows... what could say "I'm intelligent, open-minded, cultured, and liberal" more than watching a subtitled cop show from a country no one's ever been to? And then there was the bicycle scene, which sent self-satisfied cyclists into raptures over their impressive network of cycle paths, the green wave traffic lights that allow riders who travel at an average speed of 12 mph to never get caught by a red light, and the statistic that in Copenhagen there are over five bikes on the road for every car.

The cycling bores queue up like pigs in line at a Jutland slaughterhouse, ready to inundate you with facts you simply can't live without. "Did you know that in 24 hours over 750,000 miles are cycled in Copenhagen?" they trill. "When I was having dinner at Noma, my Danish friend told me that every day more than one-third of journeys are taken by bike." You can almost physically see the bulge in men's trousers as they regale you with images that they have seen on the Copenhagen Cycle Chic blog of the pretty blonde girls in floaty summer dresses riding beach cruisers. And then there's the families on bikes. "You see them all riding together: father and mother with two young children sat at the front in a trailer. They don't even feel the need to wear helmets, it's that safe!" Finally, they will out the big guns, the stat to end all stats, the one that truly fills them with glee. "The most insane thing is, in Copenhagen alone, more people commute by bicycle than in the whole of the United States. It's just SO much more civilized over there."

"Bullshit!" you reply, but they have proof… "It's on Wikipedia, check it if you want." So there you have it, a rock-solid argument if ever there was one. And then you wonder to yourself, "If the cycle scene is so great over there, why don't you do us all a favor and fuck off to wonderful Copenhagen as fast as your bike will carry you?!"

ECO WARRIOR

Unless you've been living as a hermit in a forest in Maine or work as an executive for a multinational car company, you'll be in little doubt that the human race has been treating the planet pretty poorly for the last couple of centuries. Conscious of the issues we face, a group of environmental activists have put their heads together and come up with a credible solution to global warming: riding bikes.

As a means of transport cycling is perfect. No engine means no fuel, which means no need for drilling, fracking, or refining the planet, and this also means no pollution. You've got to hand it to the environmentalists; it's a pretty convincing argument to present against the use of cars.

However, the argument falls down when faced with wan-looking vegans who've spent the last few years subsisting on a diet of self-righteousness and fair-trade soy lattes, demanding you immediately turn your back on the evils of motor vehicles and buy a bike this instant. Determined to make you see the error of your ways, they thrust into your hand leaflets printed with ink made from natural plant dyes that detail the benefits of cycling. You are pointed in the direction of websites where you can find out how a bike rider can travel over 600 miles on the energy equivalent of just one liter of petrol, or where you can buy bicycles made of sustainable bamboo costing nearly two grand. The worst thing you can do is feign polite interest—they'll think you're a kindred spirit and do their damnedest to convince you to donate some money or join them on the next protest ride against the evil oil companies.

One of the main methods eco warriors use to try and convert you to their cause is guilt. No one particularly likes to be told how they should live, so making people feel bad about something as small-scale as driving to the local store once a week is not the way forward. Yes, we understand that cycling is going to help the environment; we also realize that regular colonic irrigation and a diet consisting of no sugar, milk, fat, red meat, or carbohydrates is going to make us healthier and save all the cute little lambs, calves, and piglets. The problem is that we like steaks just as much as we like being able to drive to the shop to buy a tub of Ben and Jerry's when we can't be bothered to walk. We know it's wrong, but we're going to do it anyway, so leave us alone. And, if the world is going to hell in a handcart in 200 years' time, it doesn't matter to us because we're already dead!

Eco Warrior

DRINK & RIDER

It's approaching midnight, and the door of the bar swings open. A mumbled farewell echoes into the night and out stumbles the drunk cyclist, blinking as his eyes get used to the bright neon glow of the takeaway sign on the opposite side of the road. He scans the nearby railings and scratches his head, trying to remember where he locked his bike.

A minute or two of staggering around like a disorientated pensioner later, he locates his steed and fumbles around the bottom of his backpack in search of the key for his lock. Eventually he finds it, puts down his can of lukewarm beer, manages to release the cable attaching the bike to the railing, and puts his drunken backside on the saddle. After several aborted attempts to master the art of balancing on two wheels, he sets off with a swagger—a hammered one that is, most certainly not a bullish one—and proceeds to make the close acquaintance of a nearby tree trunk.

While watching an inebriated dickhead fall head over heels into the waiting gutter can be hilarious—in fact, Lindsey Lohan and Pete Doherty have both made moderately successful careers out of doing just that—it can also be pretty dangerous when a bike is involved. For all the (often justifiable) complaining cyclists do to assert their rights on the road and make their lives safer in the face of heavyweight motorized opposition, there's a group of riders who seem oblivious to the fact that drunkeness and cycling are not a good mix. They see nothing ironic about riding to the bar decked out head-to-toe in hi-vis clothing, resembling a pilled-up Nineties' trance raver, and then smashing back six or more pints of beer before cycling home. As they swerve from one side of the road to the other, all sense of mortality is put to the compartment of the brain labeled: "Do not use when choosing to behave like an irrational tool." You have to wonder what other examples of idiocy these people are capable of. Not pulling down the safety bar on a looping rollercoaster perhaps? Or maybe heading out for a swim when the beach has been closed due to an influx of highly toxic jellyfish? Whatever their reasoning, it's pretty clear that it's not the most sensible idea they've ever had.

As a cyclist you are in quite a vulnerable position. The body is built up of numerous parts that can be damaged when you fall and going out of your way to increase this possibility is pretty counterintuitive. Bones tend to snap easily when connecting with a fast-moving car, while teeth like to make a bid for freedom from the tyrannical clutches of the jawbone when introduced with considerable force to an immovable object like a brick wall. Sadly, the skin doesn't fair much better, tearing like cheap toilet paper when rubbed against the abrasive properties of concrete and tarmac. So, although the bike might save you time getting to bed after a night on the beers, it'll take you a lot longer to shuffle home on a set of crutches after you've gone over the handlebars and into the nearest ditch.

SECURITY EXPERT

It's a sad truth that if you leave your precious bike unattended for an extended period of time, some knuckle-dragging miscreant will be only too happy to relieve you of your property.

The time required for the theft to take place is somewhat linked to the population density of the area you are in. If you live in a tiny town where someone digging a hole in the road makes the front page of the local paper, it's probably safe to leave your bike outside the local bar overnight without having to worry too much. On the other hand, in a city full of people, unless you're known in town as someone with "family connections" (and when was the last time you saw a gangster movie where the main characters rode round on fixies?), you're taking a gamble leaving your bike outside unprotected, even if it is only for a few seconds while you pop in to Starbucks for your morning macchiato. And while the barista is asking for your name to write on the cup, the kid outside in the tracksuit is riding down the street on your pride and joy.

With the average cyclist well aware of these risks, it's up to him or her to protect their bike as best they can. For some, this involves buying a sturdy D-lock or chain, threading it through the frame and rear wheel, and securing it to something solid and immovable. For others, it's a little more complex…

Rather than take any chances, the security expert will first stake out an area to see if it's suitable for the task of locking a bike. Like espionage experts looking for the perfect place to make a drop, he searches for open spaces with lots of people, where he can leave his bike in full view of several CCTV cameras, store security guards, and passing police cars. Once he's identified an appropriate spot, the next step is to find something capable of withstanding 10 tonnes of pressure from a car jack. Easier said than done. Thirty minutes later the cyclist dismounts, puts down a backpack, and proceeds to remove a selection of heavy-duty D-locks in various sizes, each rated a maximum 5 stars by insurance companies. Next come lengths of chain sourced online from South African militiamen that are guaranteed to resist any attack from bolt cutters. Don't be concerned by the fact that each chain weighs 20lb, has caused the rider irreparable back pain, and costs more than the bike itself; no thief is getting through this.

Like a lycra-clad spider, the rider weaves an intricate chain web around the bike until little of the frame is visible. Now it's on to the saddle, and ball bearings are carefully glued into holes where Allen keys could potentially be used to remove the seat. Next, tires are deflated to foil any attempts at a quick getaway. The rider then surveys his work for weak points, takes out a phone, and photographs the bike from six different angles to ensure the bike's position has been recorded via GPS for tracking purposes. Happy that the bike is unstealable, he then heads off to the bar to meet friends. Sadly, they left an hour ago, thinking their friend, already two hours late due to a lack of suitable locking locations, was a no-show.

BIKE THIEF

I like a challenge: that's why I got into the bike thieving game, as it seemed like a good opportunity to test myself. It's nothing to do with the crack habit I've got—though admittedly that does get a little costly at times, but for the most part it's under control—I just enjoy the buzz of thieving bikes from innocent people.

The main reason I like pinching rides is because it's easy. You won't believe what some people consider to be locking up their bike... a piece of plastic that's about as thick as the wrist of an undernourished fashion model is going to put up about as much resistance to my bolt cutters as a soaking wet cigarette paper. Still, folks leave their bikes out there attached to railings by the security world's equivalent of a piece of string and are surprised

when they find I've nabbed it. But even those who spend a bit more on their locks aren't safe from me. A few years ago, there was a lock that boasted how it was completely unbreakable. They were right, it was, but I didn't need to break it as I just stuck a pen in the keyhole and it popped right open. Unbelievable, but that's a true story. It was like all us bike thieves' Christmases had come all at once, and all you bike riders' Christmas presents were coming home with us!

It's not all fun and games, though. Have you ever tried walking round town with a massive pair of bolt cutters tucked down your trouser leg? It's not easy, I can tell you, limping around like John Wayne playing a one-legged pirate. And all these CCTV cameras, God they're annoying. As soon as you do so much as even look at a bike, there'll be a camera swiveling into action like you've just walked on stage to audition for *The X-Factor*. And then, someone almost as irritating as Simon Cowell turns up, the security guard, which means I have to make a swift exit, swinging my legs so fast I look like a clockwork tin soldier. But, for all the trials and tribulations, there's always that person who only locks their quick-release wheel to the bike stand and I'm off with their ride faster than you can say, "That's my bike you thieving c***!"

I do get abused quite a lot and I have to confess it does hurt. People say I'm a scumbag, but I'm a nice guy, really. I have a lot of sympathy for the tax man and the traffic warden—we're only trying to earn a living. Deep down we're all the same, just wanting to be loved. I will admit it can't be that nice an experience to come back to find your pride and joy being ridden down the road by a gang of teenage tearaways. But then, again, a job's a job and someone's got to keep the bike lock industry in business. Without us there'd be no need for security devices and there'd be lay-offs left, right, and center. In these tricky financial times no one wants to see that, do they? So, consider it a public service and thank me later.

LOCAL BIKE SHOP OWNER

Look, I'm not going lie, I really do struggle to hide my disdain for some customers; they just don't understand bikes. I started riding when I was four years old and have never stopped. I've dedicated over 30 years of my life to cycling, not to mention spending thousands of my own hard-earned cash setting up my store. So, when some fat idiot comes in telling me he's just been watching the Tour de France and fancies giving it a go, I struggle to hide my contempt.

I'm not prepared to waste energy sharing my expert knowledge with some suit who's going to buy a bike, use it for a couple of weeks at the most, and then leave it outside to rust. If they ask me a question, I'll answer it, but I'm not going any further than that. I had a girl in the other day who asked me what the difference was between a mountain bike and a road bike. I said if you don't know that, then I don't want you in my shop, and then I politely told her to remove herself from my premises before I threw her out. She asked if the words "customer service" meant anything to me. I told her I wished birth control had meant something to her parents, before frightening her out of the shop with a few carefully aimed sprays of GT-85.

My friends ask me if business is good. Well, I'll tell you, the business of selling bikes to idiots is great, but it breaks my heart. There are still some good folk out there. I've got loads of time for them. We talk about the good old days, when riders did it for the right reasons: to race. None of this environment bollocks, thanks very much—I couldn't give a shit about that. I want to sell bikes to real men, not some idiot looking to buy a fixie to impress his mates. I stopped stocking fixed gears when all the hipsters got hold of them. I couldn't bear to betray my principles—a track bike's for the track, not for poncing about in moustaches and skinny jeans.

I run a repair service but, honestly, it makes me question the future of mankind. People let their bikes get in an utter state, then bring them to me and say they're not working. I'm not bloody surprised, your chain is disgusting! They ask me how much it's going to cost. Ha! How the hell am I supposed to know, I haven't had a proper look at it yet, you dick!

My shop sponsored a team for a while, as I wanted to give something back to the sport I love, but I soon knocked it on the head. The kids weren't good enough—they didn't have the passion. If you're not going to put your heart and soul into cycling, I'm not interested in giving you a free inner tube or discounted pair of bib shorts. Kids these days just aren't prepared to give everything, no passion whatsoever.

DRAFTER

You'd be forgiven for thinking that cycling and lazy people are two things that wouldn't get together, but you'd be wrong. There's a phenomenon that affects many aspects of cycling, from the pro peloton at the top, all the way down to the humble commuter: drafting.

The laws of physics decree that if a cyclist can tuck in close enough behind another rider, he or she can experience the sensation of slipstreaming, or drafting, whereby the person out in front shelters the follower from the wind. So, to put it in layman's terms, if you can't be arsed to put in any effort, simply sit behind another rider and let him do all the work. Then, once your free ride starts to tire and slow down, you can emerge from his wake and nonchalantly make your way past him without breaking into a sweat.

For bike racers, there's a logic to drafting. If, as a team, you take can it in turns to ride at the front and take the strain, you will work together to share the load and all benefit equally as you can maintain a higher average speed for longer. Such levels of cooperation and teamwork are enough to bring a tear to Karl Marx's eye, God rest his soul. On the other hand, if you are just a lethargic fucker who has spied an opportunity to put one's proverbial feet up, you might find you're about as welcome as a Moët-quaffing banker on an anti-capitalist march.

So, what to do when you unexpectedly find a wheel-sucking leech behind you with his nose inches away from your backside? Well, here are a few options:

1. Ignore him, as you dislike confrontation, and hope he'll go away. This is also known as the British Method.

2. Increase your speed and try to shake him from off your tail like dog shit from a shoe.

3. Channel your inner skunk and let out a particularly potent airborne toxic event that will engulf your pursuer's nostrils, leaving him struggling for breath and forced to drop back.

4. Brake suddenly. Granted this is a risky maneuver, as the force of a head impacting with your arse at high speed could leave you walking like Charlie Chaplin for weeks after the incident. But a well-executed slowing down could shock the person behind into realizing he is pushing his luck.

5. Lead him toward a hazard in the road, like a pothole or a traffic cone, and, while he is busy studying the stitching on your shorts, you can swerve at the last possible second and smile as he goes flying.

6. Turn round, tell him in no uncertain terms to back off, and watch as his face turns bright crimson, having been caught out for being such a lazy bastard.

SLOW COACH

If there's one person any self-respecting cyclist doesn't want to be, it's the slow coach. Being the rider who is always at the back of the group, squirming in the saddle as you try to catch up, is one of cycling's most demoralizing experiences. During a ride where you spend the vast majority of your time squinting at the other riders in the distance, you go through six stages of emotion. Here they are:

1. Denial: In spite of the fact that it soon becomes patently clear that you are not as fast as your fellow riders, you put in the effort to keep up. You join in on conversations, trying to hide the fact you're slightly out of breath, despite having only ridden a couple of miles, and spend a bit of time at the front of the pack, helping to set a pace you can't possibly keep.

2. Concern: "I don't know what's wrong with me, I'm just not feeling it today," you think, as you try to bridge the gap between you and the guy in front. "Maybe I need some food?"

3. Despair: Panic sets in; you know you're not up to the task. Those in front have barely broken a sweat, yet you're gasping for air and you haven't even reached the first incline. You shift through the gears, trying to find one that feels comfortable, but it's impossible. Like a cycling Goldilocks you try a higher gear... too hard. You shift down and your legs spin wildly... too easy. Sadly, you're never going to find a ratio that's just right.

4. Hatred: The first hill was seriously hard work, but the second, where every pedal stroke felt like you were being stabbed in the thighs, has really got you mad. You hate yourself for going out for a few beers last night, for being too lazy to have ridden for a month. You hate hills; in fact, you loathe them. You hate cycling in general: it's expensive, it's dangerous, it's time-consuming, but, most of all, it's fucking hard work. And then you start to hate those ahead of you. They're out of sight now, waiting for you at the top of the climb, the arrogant bastards. They say well done when you reach them, how dare those patronizing chumps! And then they say the words that make you, having exhausted every ounce of energy you had in your body, want to strangle them, but you can't muster the strength… "Right, shall we crack on?"

5. Hope: You hope you're nearing the end of the ride. You hope that you've done more miles than you thought. You hope that the group ahead is starting to tire. You hope that someone ahead has gone too big, too early and you'll no longer be the one at the back. But, most of all, you hope that there are no more of those bastard hills.

6. Resignation: You give in, you're not going to keep up, so you've got little choice than to grit your teeth and get on with it. Sure, there are over 30 miles to go, but, if you go at your own pace, you can do it. And, next time you decide to go for a ride with your mates, you'll make sure you're a damn sight better prepared.

TOURER

For many, a week or two off work is the ideal opportunity to switch off from the stresses and strains of the daily grind and relax. This could involve days spent lying on a beach, leisurely afternoon walks in the countryside, or nights spent forcing as much cheap food and booze as humanly possible into a continuously expanding stomach... all perfectly reasonable ways to unwind. For others it could involve a buttock-and-back-destroying cycling odyssey, riding at least 70 miles every day, while loaded down with a week's worth of luggage and supplies like a long-suffering pack animal.

The tourer's motto is: "A trip not taken by bike is a trip not worth doing." In this era of modern travel, where package deals are cheaper than ever before, the tourer chooses to ignore offers of a low-cost week relaxing by the pool in favor of seven days of hard cycling. Sun beds are swapped for saddle sore, lilos replaced by lactic acid build-up, and local gastronomic delights are eschewed in favor of energy gels and isotonic drinks. For these riders, the benefit in the explosion of low-cost flights is not the ability to experience new cities or beaches on the cheap, but the chance to take the bike to hotter climes and up hillier climbs. And, once they've finished the tour, the final day can be spent in search of a cycle shop who are kind enough to give them a cardboard box that they can pack their bike in ready for the flight back home. What fun.

If this is how a solo cycle-lover or like-minded group of enthusiasts wish to enjoy their vacation, who are we to judge? But when an entire family are expected to forego a pleasant few days doing nothing in particular in favor of riding up mountains in blazing sunshine or down them in torrential rain, it doesn't seem quite so reasonable. Children return to school after the summer break with a glazed expression, and, after hearing about their classmates' trips to the seaside or fun-packed visits to theme parks and museums, they recount in a hollow voice how their parents forced them to ride for four hours down a dual carriageway in a hail storm to make it to that evening's designated campsite before sunset.

The kids of touring enthusiasts are told they'll look back at these special family moments and treasure them. Perhaps in a similar way to how that painful evening at Grandma and Grandpa's 40th wedding anniversary, where you were repeatedly pinched on the cheek and kissed on the lips by countless aging relatives who smelt mildly of antiseptic, also represented quality family time.

---

no. 25

CLIMBER

Cycling is a sport defined by gravity. From a very young age you soon learn that going downhill is fun, as it takes very little effort and you can go really fast, but going uphill is an absolute pain in the neck and should be avoided at all costs. Everybody knows this, so why some people claim that they love hills is beyond the comprehension of most rational people.

The climber would beg to differ. Weighing in at less than your average 12-year-old girl and blessed with a physique that would make even a starving Ethiopian child feel sympathy for his apparent lack of nourishment, he rides up hills on bikes that are so light you worry they might be blown away if the wind picks up. These pigeon-chested peddlers are cyclists that irritate the hell out of their fellow riders. On TV they are a joy to watch, flying up inhuman gradients at unbelievable speeds, but when one powers past as you force yourself up a short climb—bidding you a cheery hello as you struggle for breath—you really wish them ill.

When the climber plans routes for rides with friends, this masochist will throw in a few steep hills to the ride, just for a bit of "fun." That's fun in the absolute loosest sense of the word, unless your idea of a good time is spent huffing, puffing, and cursing your way up a stretch of road that rises from sea level to 1300ft in just a couple of miles. At the top of such a hill, the climber will be waiting for you, ready to tell you how much he enjoyed that. Surely he must be lying; he's the type of disingenuous person who claims he'd rather eat a salad than a steak, or says he used to watch Baywatch solely for the plotlines. You, on the other hand, are ready to advise the skinny bastard to ride down the hill you've just conquered and straight into the first passing car if he thinks you're crazy enough to do something like that again.

At home, the climber likes nothing more than spending time researching the biggest hills and the steepest gradients in his area, determined to master them all. Once that's done, he'll look further afield, planning holidays around mountain passes, tricking loved ones into heading to remote, incredibly dull places, just so that he can spend five days out of a week-long holiday defying gravity and common sense, ticking off each climb on his list of 100 hills to do before you die... or your knees pack up.

SOMMET MONT VENTOUX
(Alt 1912 m)

Despite his considerable talents at defying the laws of gravity and destroying anyone who decides to join him for an undulating ride, the climber can still struggle to win bike races. If the course involves pretty much solid climbing for 100 miles, he'll be top of his game, but, if it involves any kind of speed or show of muscular power, he gets blown away. And all the riders blessed with bigger frames will take great delight in doling out their own form of punishment to these uphill upstarts.

SPRINTER

The rider, incandescent with rage, threw his helmet at the window of the team bus. Those team mates unfortunate enough to be in the immediate vicinity of the impact zone flinched as shards of plastic shrapnel bounced off the glass and tiny polystyrene specs floated through the air like synthetic flakes of snow. The rider walked over to the Nespresso machine he'd personally requested in his contract—he loved his coffee, you see— and made himself an espresso to calm his nerves.

"How dare they? How fucking dare they?" he screamed at nobody in particular. "To even suggest I altered from the racing line is absolute bullshit. I've been sprinting for over 10 years, putting my neck on the line. I *am* bike racing. Journalists haven't got the slightest clue. Those keyboard warriors just sit on Twitter all day, bitching and moaning, talking shit about me and then spewing their venom onto the cycling websites. They could never achieve what I have."

Blessed with a talent that could only be matched by his considerable ego and desire to win, Matt Bradshaw was one of the most gifted sprinters in the history of cycling. He was also one of the most temperamental. Having burst onto the pro tour from almost out of nowhere, this sprint phenomenon had wowed the cycling fraternity during his first year on Team Freewave by picking up four stage wins at cycling's blue riband event, the Tour of Europe. Five years later and he's proved himself to be unbeatable, until today.

Bradshaw got up from his leather seat and motioned toward the door in the middle of the bus. Outside, just a few feet away, waited a large gaggle of journalists. They all hoped to get a quote from the man they'd dubbed the Pint-sized Projectile on account of his short stature, yet powerful perfomances.

"Don't go out there, please," pleaded Team Freewave's director of communications. He'd seen Matt like this on several occasions. "Just take some time to calm down before you go and talk to them."

"Screw you," was the succinct response.

The journalists, sensing some movement behind the tinted glass, stopped discussing the day's events and moved their hands down to beside their pockets. They were ready to

unsheathe their microphones and recording devices at a moment's notice, keen to do battle with an irate Bradshaw baying for media blood.

There was a hiss of hydraulics and, like the scene in a sci-fi movie where the alien comes out of his spaceship for the first time, the door slowly opened to reveal the formidable opponent. Bradshaw eyed the group with disdain and slowly, purposefully walked toward the cluster of recording equipment being thrust in his direction.

"Matt, reports are coming in that Dieter is blaming you for the crash. He's in the hospital getting an X-ray now. They think it might be his collarbone," shouted one of the reporters from German television.

"You know what, I'd like to take Dieter Reinhardt's collarbone and shove it up his ass. He's cost me a win today, he deserves everything he gets," Bradshaw snapped back. "This whole day has been a massive balls-up from start to finish. My team was not good enough and the support I require wasn't there. Next thing I know Globo Sunnyday are out at the front of the peloton taking unnecessary risks, looking for gaps that aren't there, trying to get on my wheel."

"Do you not think it's fair for the riders from Globo to say the same thing about you?" countered the cycling correspondent from Dutch radio. At this point you could almost see the smoke about to come out of Bradshaw's ears and the vein by his right temple rapidly swelled and pulsed like an earthworm being poked and prodded by a couple of bored teenagers. The media scrum suddenly fell silent, their instinctive fight or flight responses were kicking into action, putting all their senses on red alert. The Pint-sized Projectile was about to go nuclear.

"You fucking what?" screeched Bradshaw. "What's your name? No, wait, don't tell me. I never want to hear your voice ever again. Leave this race now before I tear out your intestines and use them for inner tubes." With this frankly bizarre threat, he ripped the Dutch journalist's tape recorder out of her hand and, struggling to find a way to express his highly emotional state, placed it into his mouth and bit down on the plastic casing. For the next five minutes, the world's cycling media watched in stunned silence as Bradshaw, arguably the greatest sprinter ever to have pedaled a bike, proceeded to attempt to eat a Dictaphone.

Twenty-four hours later and Matt Bradshaw is grinning like a Cheshire cat. Twenty minutes ago he won his 26th stage of the Tour of Europe, placing him in third place on the all-time list of stage winners. He now stood in front of a television camera, being interviewed by Ed Colton from British TV. "That was a fantastic performance today, Matt. Tell me about it."

"The team today were incredible, just incredible. It was tough out there, but they gave everything for me. I'm so, so grateful for all their hard work. They were totally committed today, I'm speechless. And I have to give credit to Dieter Reinhardt, he's one of the best sprinters out there, he pushes me hard every time. He's a great bike handler and an incredible competitor. He'll no doubt pick up a few stage wins himself soon."

What a difference a day makes.

CLUB RIDER

Most people's idea of a relaxing weekend morning is a long lie-in, perhaps a spot of brunch, some good conversation, and a leisurely read through the morning papers. It certainly isn't getting up at the crack of dawn to meet up with a gang of like-minded road warriors, all dressed up like a troop of power rangers, before heading out for several hours of physical exertion.

Every Saturday and Sunday, come rain or shine, members of cycling clubs across the known world will gather at a prearranged point, before splitting into groups based on speed and ability to climb up a hill. This is to ensure that the finely tuned athletes of the club don't risk giving the other members a coronary as they try to keep up. The various packs then head out, the keener riders to do some serious training, the more social members to head for a café several miles down the road to stop for a coffee and a catch-up, which represents cycling's equivalent of downing a few beers after a football game.

The link between cycling, club rides, and coffee is a long one, and, as older members of a club will no doubt tell you, the origins possibly stem from Faema, an Italian company that makes espresso machines, sponsoring a cycling team during the Sixties, which included one Eddy Merckx. They may not be so quick to admit that stopping for coffee also gives riders the excuse to shove a piece of sweet, sugary cake into their mouths, using the excuse that they've just had a strenuous workout to justify having another slice.

Club riders are the heart and soul of the competitive cycling world. This is where younger riders learn their craft, athletes train for races, born-again cyclists get to live out their pro-peloton aspirations by riding in formation, and where MAMILs (see page 18) get to socialize with fellow mid-life-crisis riders who love riding ultra-light, carbon-fiber bikes almost as much as they enjoy talking about them. Unfortunately, some clubs also have a reputation for being notoriously cliquey and wary of interlopers who don't know their derailleur from their domestique. Still, don't let these people, with heads almost as far up their own arses as the chamois pad of their cycling shorts, put you off. If you want to ride regularly with a group of fellow bike enthusiasts, or simply want to satisfy your weekly craving for caffeine and baked goods, there are a lot worse places you can be.

STRAVAHOLIC

Cell phones and bicycles are seemingly disparate devices but, since the advent of the smart phone, the two have become inextricably linked. Whether it's the GPS capabilities which highlight where you are on a map or the apps that show you, step by step, how to fix a rear derailleur, the phone is never far from a rider's reach.

Recently, one of the most popular apps to appeal to the cycling fan is Strava, the program that lets you record your rides and compare your performances against other cyclists. By using a feature called segments, riders are able to program in a particular stretch of road—say a hill that is ridden up regularly or a long straight street on the daily commute—and Strava will then record the time and speed of any user who uses the same section of tarmac. The cyclist who rides up the segment the fastest is then awarded the title of King of the Mountains, a reward that matters very little in the grand scheme of things but, for some, this recognition is everything.

The Stravaholic's first foray into segments is innocent enough. After hearing fellow cycling buddies talking about it, the user will set up an account under a hilarious alter-ego that only fellow cycling geeks would get—something along the lines of Pelo-Tom or the Velo-ciraptor would be perfect. He'll then record a few rides and see how he's doing. Initial reactions are good, he enjoys the way it adds an element of excitement to his journey to work, and it is gratifying to see how his performances are improving. Soon Strava awards him his first trophy, presented for beating a previous time, and that's it, he's hooked.

A constant desire to push that little bit harder, to go that little bit faster, to earn more trophies, and to jump a few places up the leaderboard is hard for the Stravaholic to resist. But, what started out as a bit of fun soon becomes an obsession, with the app junkie instantly uploading his ride performances as soon as he reaches his final destinations. Any time that the rider is not able to go out for a ride is spent nervously checking the phone to see if his rivals have taken the opportunity to steal a march while he's been out of action.

Not content with a position of 100th out of 1,500 on the "Main Street Lung Popper," the rider starts to specifically target this segment. Initially, he rides slowly for the first part of his journey to conserve energy and hit the segment start-point at full pelt. This results in a slightly higher standing on the leaderboard, but it's not good enough. The Stravaholic has heard about the aggregation of marginal gains technique employed by some of cycling's top teams, so looks to analyze the factors affecting his performance in order to improve half a percent here, a quarter of a percent there. He peels stickers from his bike frame, he shaves his legs, he doesn't wear socks, he buys an all-in-one speed suit. All these adjustments will soon add up to an improved performance, so he's told. He spends time sat by the side of the road monitoring the traffic light sequences to establish when he's least likely to get caught at a red. He also records the times when there are fewer cars to block his path.

These little tweaks help him make significant time gains and soon he's in the top ten. Result! But there's still a bit more to go. His solution is a carefully controlled diet and three-week period of high-intensity training both on the bike and at the gym, followed by a ten-day tapering period. After the tenth day, he's ready. He wakes up, fixes himself a breakfast of proteins and quick-release carbohydrates, then puts his bike in the car and drives to the segment start-point. He stretches and prepares himself for the start. The lights change from red to green, and he's off. Forty-three seconds later he crosses the end-point. He slams on the breaks and immediately uploads the ride. He looks at the time—it's his best yet. He looks at the leaderboard. He's top and the newly crowned King of the Mountains.

For the next few days he's on cloud nine; it's been a long time since he felt so good. And then, suddenly, his world is turned upside down. His iPhone beeps, it's an alert from Strava: his KOM status has been lost, someone's beaten him. Incredulous, he checks the details: someone has completed the segment at 37 mph. His speed was 27 mph. It then slowly dawns on him: this time wasn't done on a bike, it was done in a car. He's furious, all his hard work undone by a cheat. He instantly emails Strava to have the time removed and his reinstated, but the messages remain unanswered. And, just like that, all his hard work is for nothing. He's King of the Mountains, but nobody knows it other than him.

ALL THE GEAR, NO IDEA

Be prepared is the motto taught at a young age to anyone who decides to join the Scout Movement, and this mantra has stuck with a certain type of person throughout his life. The sort of person who, whenever he takes up a new hobby or develops a new interest, feels the need to throw everything he has (i.e. cash) at his current favorite pastime.

The financier decided to dip a toe, or rather fully submerge himself balls deep, into the metaphorical waters of cycling after realizing he needed to shape up, following a humiliating last place in the three-legged race at his son's sports day. And it had to be cycling because tennis was out of the question after he was banned from his local country club following a regrettable incident last year at the club's annual championship when an over-zealous umpire called his serve out when it was clearly in. The official has never walked quite the same way since.

He remembered a conversation he'd had with a colleague at the bank one morning, as they shared a lift up to the trading floor. The associate in question had cycled into the office and was extolling the virtues of riding: he felt healthier, the journey was quicker, he felt more awake, he was losing weight etc, etc. Needless to say, All the Gear's interest was piqued.

And so, the banker found himself in a fancy city bike shop, the kind where they don't put prices on anything because,

if you have to ask, you can't afford it. He was being measured up for a carbon-fiber Specialized Venge. The exact same model that Mark Cavendish used, the sales assistant informed him. All the Gear thought he recognized the name, Cav worked in mergers and acquisitions if he wasn't mistaken—clearly he's also a keen cyclist. All the Gear seemed to remember sharing a bottle of Pomerol with him at the Christmas party, nice guy. The salesman asked if he wanted to take the bike out for a test ride to see if it was a good fit, but he was late for his next meeting, so he signed the check for an obscene amount of money and wheeled the bike out of the store and back to the office.

The next day he remembered his co-worker's outfit and decided he had to look the part if he was going to ride. After a morning spent shouting at the legal department, ATG went back to the bike store to get kitted out in the finest Rapha, Sidi, and Assos cycle apparel money could buy. The guy in the store told him it was the best, so he bought it without hesitation. There was no way he was going to head out on a ride dressed like an amateur.

That weekend ATG planned to cycle over to Richmond Park, a spot not too far from his west London home that he'd heard was popular with other city riders. He put on his new outfit, struggled with the ratchet bindings on his new cycling shoes, and threw a mighty leg over the tube of his new ride. ATG pressed the button to open the electronic gate at the front of his six-bedroom home and tentatively pulled out of the drive onto the sidewalk. After all, there was no way he was going to risk his life riding on the road.

Initially, ATG wobbled a little, trying to keep his balance. "Why the hell did they make the pedals on this bike so small?" he pondered. A few hundred yards later and he was getting the hang of it. "It's true what they say, you never forget."

A little further along, he encountered his first hill and looked to change gears, but couldn't see the index shifters he recalled from his school days on either the handlebars or the down tube. The modern STI shifters integrated with the brakes were lost on him. "This bike is a piece of junk, all that money and there's only one gear," he fumed as he struggled up the slope.

Eventually, ATG reached the top and, after yelling at a few pensioners to get out of his way, he started picking up speed as he began the descent. This was more like it. Suddenly, out of nowhere, a dog ran out from an open door and directly into his path. ATG panicked and did the only thing he could think of to avoid hitting the mutt. He slammed on his ultra-responsive Shimano Dura Ace front brake, which did its job admirably and stopped the bike dead in its tracks. Sadly, ATG's momentum launched him gracefully into the air, his black-and-white kit making him bear more than a passing resemblance to the escape scene in *Free Willy*. Inevitably, face met concrete with a powerful thud, leaving ATG with cuts to his face and hands, a nasty bruise on his hip, and a battered sense of pride.

Dejectedly, ATG wheeled his bike back to the house, wincing in pain at every torturous step. Once home he pressed the button to open up his electric garage door and positioned the bike alongside the golf clubs, barbecue, tennis racket, cross trainer, rowing machine, and snowboard, never to be used again.

ZERO TO HERO

Chances are, if you're the type of person whose idea of physical exertion is trying to get the plastic wrapping off the top of a microwave curry, you'll have very little interest in cycling. On the other hand, there are those of you who, following a trip to the doctor where you're told that if you don't get your oversized backside off the sofa and do some exercise, you're in danger of doing a James Gandolfini, decide to laugh in the face of death and do the unthinkable. You buy a bike.

As you get ready for your first ride, you catch a glimpse of yourself in the mirror and are disappointed by the fact that you're about to do the one thing you always swore you wouldn't: you're going to exercise. The first few rides are literally hell on earth, not only physically, but also mentally, as you have to endure kids laughing at you, adults pitying you, and pensioners with zimmer frames traveling faster than you. But wait, after a few attempts, you notice things start to get easier, there's an improvement in your performance and you don't feel like your heart's going to explode like Mr. Creosote every time you shift into a bigger gear. Soon, the regular loop around the park becomes a cinch, and you're cycling the few miles to the office. Next comes the first 10 mile ride, then the 20 mile one, and, within a few months, you've found yourself signed up for your first century ride—that's 100 miles!

Now, while all this is great for your health, you can't help but feel a real sense of betrayal as you realize you've become the embodiment of everything you previously hated. In the past, you and your fellow big-boned brethren sneered at the active and laughed at people who watched their weight. How could they possibly enjoy going for a run when they could be sat playing *Call of Duty* and gorging on bucketfuls of fried chicken instead? And yet, much like the compulsion to dial for pizza was hard to ignore, so too is the desire to cycle further and faster than you've ever managed before.

You are justifiably incredibly proud of your achievements: your friends compliment you, members of the opposite sex now notice you, and the neighbors in the apartment below thank you for no longer waking them up in the middle of the night by stomping across the ceiling when you need to take a leak. Nevertheless, in quiet moments of contemplation, there's still that part of you that questions whether the enjoyment of devouring a box of a dozen Krispy Kremes, washed down with a gallon of Dr Pepper, really wouldn't be better than another five years of life.

SOFA CYCLIST

Watching paint dry is often held up as the ultimate in boring activities, but being forced to sit through an entire 120-mile bike race is enough to test the patience of all but the most comatose of personalities. In fact, if a viewer hasn't been tempted to change the channel after the third hour of a race, you'd do well to check to make sure they haven't ended it all rather than be forced to watch another ascent of some hill some bloke went up really fast a few years ago.

Cycling on the TV is hard work; even the most committed fan would admit in quieter moments, when none of his fellow enthusiasts are around, that the first few hours of a flat stage are about as entertaining as having to suffer all seven *Fast & Furious* movies in succession. Riding a bike can be fun, but watching someone else do it is not. At least if you're out cycling, you get to focus on things other than close-ups of team cars passing water bottles to riders or commentators desperately trying to fill the time by droning on about some irrelevant landmark that the peloton has just passed by. "These cows are Friesians, a very popular breed in the area, as their milk is used by the locals on their cornflakes before they go to work each morning." Gripping, you'll no doubt agree.

Watching a race in the flesh is also pretty poor. Going to see it live consists of several hours of hanging around, followed by a minute of action, and then a long walk back to the car. And, if you're watching the contest from the comfort of your own home, it could be argued that the final five minutes of a sprint stage can be edge-of-your-seat stuff, but the other 295 minutes leading up to this are pretty much just a filler before the explosive finish. Mountain stages have the potential to offer something a bit more exciting, but, for the uninitiated, unaware of the tactics and the format of a race, the view of someone getting out of the saddle to cycle a tiny bit faster than the guy next to him is never going to go down as the most thrilling televisual event of the decade. And don't even mention the time trials. Solo riders competing against the clock... watching them on television should be prescribed to the sleep-deprived as a way to guarantee a decent night's shut-eye.

With some bike races, such as the Tour de France, Giro d'Italia, and Vuelta a España, lasting for three weeks, it's the long-suffering partners, friends, and family of cycling fans who really deserve sympathy. For it is them who have to bear the brunt of endless hours spent watching TV producers come up with increasingly tenuous ways to fill five hours of broadcasting every day. "And now we'll have a chat with a local school teacher, whose students have made a banner out of milk cartons that looks a bit like the French flag." Yawn.

HOARDER

The wife often asks me, "Do you really need all this stuff?" I just smile sweetly as she goes off on one again and hope she gets bored of the sound of her own voice. She's a real oxygen thief that one. Why she can't leave me alone to get on with scouring eBay and the bike forums for some bargains I'll never know. My hobby is building bikes, hers is moaning—different strokes for different folks, so deal with it!

I gave up riding a few years ago because of a dodgy knee, but I can't give up my bikes. At the last count I think I had something like 12 in total, with enough spare parts to put together another four or five. You might think that's a little on the excessive side, but everyone's entitled to a hobby and this is mine. Each of those bicycles means a lot to me; they're like my children. Well, my boys are more like my children, but at least this lot doesn't answer back!

We have a relatively modest home and I'll admit storage can be a bit of an issue. As a result, I keep some of them in the garage and I've managed to squeeze a few of the others into the shed. The kids, that is, not the bikes, ha! Only kidding, I'd never do that, but it has been known for me to have a clear out of my boys' rooms in order to give me a bit more space for a few bits and pieces. They don't thank me for it, but who needs one of those skateboard things anyway; a bike's much faster and the clothes you wear fit a lot better—no baggy jeans for a practical person, as you'd only get them caught in the chain.

I hope one day that my passion will rub off on the boys and they'll take an interest in bikes. So far they've resisted; for them it's all about football, but I'll keep shoving cycling in their faces until they either share my affection or move out. Either way, it's win-win for me as it means I'll either get new cycling buddies or more space to store my latest purchases.

The wife, God love her, is always in my ear to clear out my collection of jerseys—I've gathered together at least 50 over the years—or some of the boxes of bike parts from the spare room. She says it's a family home, not a repair shop, and bangs on and on about how nice it'd be to have some friends to stay for the weekend. She's right, it would be nice, but it's nicer to have somewhere to keep my collection. If she wants to see her mates, I'm happy for her to ship off and spend some quality time with them. I've got more than enough here to keep me occupied. Plus, I've just found a quality site in Italy that's selling a load of Seventies' Campagnolo parts dirt cheap, so will need somewhere to stick them. I spotted she's got a box of clothes in the bedroom wardrobe that I never see her wear, so, while she's out moaning about me, I'll bin those and stick my bike parts in there. She won't mind; after all, what you don't know about won't hurt.

HISTORIAN

Cycling has a long history, and there's nothing some enthusiasts like better than to trawl through the archives in search of gutsy riders, epic races, and weird and wonderful tales from the peloton. If it were possible, these anoraks would happily sew leather patches to tweed race jerseys and bury themselves in a pile of old cycling books rather than head out on a bike.

In a sport where the period before the Second World War is known as the heroic era, the historian doesn't have to look hard to find tales of courageous feats of daring, stories of sabotage, and incredible examples of endurance, and will regale anyone who'll give him the time of day with stories of superhuman strength, unrivaled cunning, and disgraceful skulduggery.

The Tour de France alone has generated enough material to fill hundreds of books. *La Grande Boucle* was created by sadist Henri Desgrange, a man who liked nothing more than conjuring up near-impossible routes to challenge competitors. In his eyes, if riders were able to complete a race, it wasn't hard enough and he developed increasingly devious ways to make riders suffer... an almost 7,000-ft climb up a mountain that's barely passable on foot and often covered with snow? Why the hell not! As a result, there are countless tales of derring-do and deception, both in equal measure. Take, for example, the legend of Eugène Christophe, who broke his fork during the 1913 Tour de France, pushed his bike 8 miles to the nearest village blacksmith, forged himself a replacement fork, and still managed to finish the race. A look at the darker side of Le Tour exposes incidents such as the 1904 edition, where nine riders were thrown out of the race for offences such as catching trains to towns closer to the finishing line. It was during this year that Frenchmen Hippolyte Aucouturier, himself no stranger to sabotage having had his water bottle spiked the previous year, decided to tie one end of a piece of string to the fender of a support vehicle and the other end to a cork. This was placed in his mouth and he was towed to four stage victories. Ingenious.

The Giro d'Italia will also have been covered in depth by this chronicler of road racing. The 1914 edition is a particular favorite, yielding facts such as the average length of a stage being an incredible 407km, that's over 250 miles a day, which meant only eight people managed to complete the challenge.

The historian's findings aren't just limited to Europe. "Did you know," he'll say, "That track cycling was once one of the biggest sports in the US and that New York's Madison Square Garden was originally used to host bike races many years before the arrival of basketball and ice hockey?"

Or, while watching a contest in which an Aussie rider is doing well, he'll bestow on you some obscure fact about the Warrnambool–Melbourne race, first held in 1895, being the world's longest one-day race at a punishing 186 miles. It's all fascinating stuff… if you have any interest in cycling. If you don't, then once collared by one of these chaps, you'll be thinking up dastardly tactics to get them to pipe down.

CYCLING NATIONS

Much like the terrain it covers, cycling has had its fair share of ups and downs over the years. While in some countries cycling is currently enjoying something of a renaissance, in other more traditional bastions of the sport, bike riding is suffering, as not only are fans left disappointed by the constant scandals that affect road racing, but people are also turning their backs on the bike as a mode of transport in favor of less energetic ways of getting from A to B. Here's a list of countries that have played an important part in the growth of cycling, both in the past and the present.

United States:

The United States has had a turbulent relationship with cycling. After an auspicious start in the late eighteenth and early nineteenth centuries, when cycling was one of the country's most popular sports, it became increasingly overlooked in the years following the Second World War. Cycling became a niche sport, and this outsider status encouraged forward-thinking—or insane, given the physical risks they were taking—riders to invent new forms of riding. California became a hotbed of counter-culture sporting endeavors and was instrumental in the development of mountain biking during the late Seventies and BMXing, which became a global phenomenon, during the Eighties. Also, during the Eighties, road racing once again captured the public's imagination, as Greg LeMond became the first American to win a stage of the Tour de France in 1985, before going on to win the race the following year and again in 1989 and 1990. In recent years, the United States managed to produce arguably the sport's only global megastar, Lance Armstrong, who propelled bikes and bike racing into the consciousness of the average man on the street. Sadly, Lance's seven Tour de France wins turned out to be about as genuine as Bill Clinton's claims he did not have an affair with Monica Lewinsky, but, so far at least, cycling still continues to grow in popularity across the country.

Belgium:

You'd be hard pressed to find a more enthusiastic group of cycling fans than the Belgians, because bike racing is one of the country's national sports. In return, cycling has done a lot to put Belgium on the map and, arguably, without the successes of superstar Eddy Merckx in the Sixties and Seventies, the only famous lowlanders Joe Public would be able to identify are the Smurfs, the bloke who wrote Tintin, and whasshisname from those terrible action movies from the Eighties where he punched people a lot. Every spring, thousands of exceptionally passionate home supporters line the streets to watch Classic races that have over 100 years of history, including Liege-Bastogne-Liege and the Tour of Flanders, happily munching on moules frites and enjoying the local beers. For these Belgians, cycling isn't a hobby, it's a way of life.

China:

Cycling became a great symbol of China and, unlike in most countries, the bike has always primarily been seen as a mode of transport rather than something that is ridden for pleasure. The fact that cycling is efficient and cost-effective has also always fitted in well with the country's socialist ideals. The image of Chinese people in conical hats cycling next to paddy fields is familiar to Westerners, but, in fact, as the Chinese economy grows and Western culture gradually worms its way into Chinese society, people are putting their bikes to one side as they aspire to own cars, which are seen as a huge signifier of prosperity. Still, just through the sheer size of the population, there are approximately 500,000,000 bikes in the country, which is a mind-boggling amount that accounts for around half the number of bikes in the whole world.

Denmark:

If you discount Lego and Lurpak, Denmark's small size means its exploits and achievements aren't often familiar to outsiders. However, if you mention the country to bike enthusiasts, they'll be able to tell you all about their excellent facilities for cyclists. Copenhagen is the envy of the world when it comes to cycling infrastructure, with visitors to the city becoming overwhelmed with nostalgic awe as they speak in reverent tones to friends back home about their experiences of the Danish capital.

France:

One of the first countries to be involved in the development of the bicycle, no nation has played a bigger role in bike racing than France, largely due to the fact that

each year it holds cycling's blue riband event, Le Tour. For most of the twentieth century, the French were obsessed with the event, putting down their glasses of pastis to watch legends like Jacques Anquetil, Louis Bobet, and Bernard Hinault claim win after win after win. At the end of the century, the French public were devastated by the Festina affair, where one of their top teams was enveloped in a doping scandal that rocked the sport. Further doping revelations and a lack of strong French riders in recent years have meant that the French public are in danger of falling out of love with bike racing, but the healthy alpine mountain bike and cyclosportive scenes mean that there are more people out on their bikes than ever. Also, the French love a winner, so, if a bright young hope emerges and manages to win Le Tour in the next decade, you can guarantee they'll be saying "Chapeau" and raising millions of glasses of vin rouge all the way from Calais to Cannes.

Holland:

Like their fellow Belgian lowlanders, the Dutch love their bike racing as much as they like bikes in general. When cycling began to decline in popularity all over the Western world, following the advent of car culture, rather than let the Dutch public put their clogs up and get lazy as they embraced the motor vehicle, successive governments had the foresight to actively encourage cycling and invested heavily in a cycling infrastructure. The policy paid off, which means that today in Holland every citizen old enough to ride has an average of 1.3 bikes to his or her name and is more than happy to ride them regularly. As a result, every member of this cycle-obsessed nation rides an average of 1½ miles a day, putting an end to the myth among unenlightened teenagers across the globe that the Dutch are all too stoned to go anywhere.

Italy:

Much as in the car industry, Italian bike brands such as Colnago, Campagnolo, and Bianchi are lauded over by cycling fans as much for their history within the sport as for their reputation for high-quality engineering.

History plays an important part in the Italian cycling world, as the Tifosi—the name given to the ultra-passionate local fans— hold up twentieth-century riders, particularly Fausto Coppi and Gino Bartali, as some of the greatest sporting heroes of all time. In recent years, this obsession with the past, while far from being uncommon in cycling, has led to disappointment among Italian fans, as they struggle to find another hero to meet their high standards. In the Nineties, a charismatic climber named Marco Pantani gave the nation hope for the future, but, sadly, his career was marred by doping controversy and his tragic death in 2004. Still, Italian riders like Vincenzo Nibali continue to dominate in the Giro in the same way that their former Prime Minister dominates the newspapers with his latest Bunga Bunga exploits. This gives the Tifosi something to cheer for, even if it's not quite as impressive as the successes they have celebrated in the past.

Spain:

Amazing landscapes, varied terrain, excellent climate, and quiet roads make Spain a paradise for many cycling fans. Whether it's the Pyrenees in the north east or the rugged mountains of Majorca or Lanzarote to the south and west, Spaniards have a wealth of opportunities to go out and test themselves, and it's where many pro riders and teams base themselves for training purposes. Over recent years, the Spanish have produced some of the greatest stage racers of the modern era, with Miguel Indurain winning five Tour de Frances in a row and Alberto Contador winning all three Grand Tours during his career—just don't mention the 2010 tour where he was stripped of his title due to an unfortunate incident with a steak dinner. On a day-to-day level, in the last year, the number of bikes bought by Spaniards overtook the number of car purchases, and, while cynics may attribute this to a weak economy, bike optimists will cheer.

United Kingdom:

The United Kingdom has a rich cycling history that goes back well into the mid-nineteenth century and, for many years, cycling was enormously popular. However, the growth of car culture in the Fifties led to a steady

decline in the number of riders taking to the road. Apart from the odd event, such as Scotsman Robert Millar's King of the Mountains victories in Le Tour and the Giro during the Eighties, as well as the emergence of world champion and Olympic gold medalist Chris Boardman as the best British rider of the Nineties, this downturn continued pretty much until the end of the century. Come the start of the new millennium and all this was about to change as, under the stewardship of performance coach Dave Brailsford, British cycling became the dominant team in track cycling, with Bradley Wiggins, Chris Hoy, Victoria Pendleton, Laura Trott, and many others winning Olympic and World titles in the velodrome. Brits have also proved to be a force to be reckoned with on the road. Mark Cavendish is arguably the greatest sprinter of all time, while Wiggins and Chris Froome have both worn cycling's greatest prize: the yellow jersey of the Tour de France. In mountain biking, both the British men's and women's teams have produced world champions as well. Given that for years Brits had very little to celebrate in terms of sporting success, many have taken cycling to their hearts, helping it to go from strength to strength.

FAIR-WEATHER CYCLIST

They say lightning never strikes twice; well, that's certainly true for the Fair-weather Cyclist. While other, more hardy, riders head out and stay out on their bike come rain or shine, this pussy bolts for cover as soon as a gray cloud appears on the horizon. The Fair-weather Cyclist likes her bike, but not enough to risk getting a soaking or the distinctly unlikely possibility of developing a nasty case of the sniffles over the next few days.

A commute to work will be nixed if the hand of the barometer has moved anywhere close to "changeable." Evening training rides will be canceled in favor of a spinning class that's safely under cover at the gym if there is even the slightest chance of precipitation. During the week before a planned ride with friends to the coast, the weather app on the iPhone is monitored continuously and real-time updates from the meteorological office are emailed on an hourly basis to keep her abreast of the situation. On the day of the ride, a flurry of text messages will be sent to fellow attendees, containing increasingly creative excuses for not venturing out in the wet. The aquaphobe has already exhausted her cache of mechanical issues and the overused cover story of a night of excessive boozing is starting to raise suspicions. Now, in order to provide the necessary subterfuge, it's up to "sick" aunts and an endless stream of family birthdays that must be attended.

It's not only the rain that strikes fear into the heart of this rider. When temperatures start to fall and the warm summer months make way for milder autumn weather, it becomes increasingly hard for her to motivate herself to get out on the bike. To give her some credit, she did once try to wrap up warm and head out in early October, but, trying to ride a bike dressed like Scott of the Antarctic, proved trickier than expected, and she ended up falling into a huge pile of ocher-tinged maple leaves.

And, when the first frosts arrive, the bike and the rider quickly retreat inside like hibernating squirrels, choosing to remain cozy and warm, rather than risk exposing an appendage to the elements. It is there they stay until the mercury once again manages to hit levels that don't require you to risk losing a limb to frostbite—otherwise known as the summer—when they tentatively set foot outside, only to spot an ominous-looking cloud, which prompts them to quickly run back inside.

ANGRY CYCLIST*

Bike riders exist in a fragile cerebral microclimate, consisting mainly of themselves, which is based on a notion of personal space. They are happy in their own world; it's a safe zone against all the other people around them. One in which they are free to think about the issues of the day or hum the song that has managed to worm its way into the subconscious that morning. (For me, it's usually some early Nineties' Euro pop, with Ace of Bass regularly making an unwelcome appearance.)

However, as soon as someone unexpectedly enters into that personal space with anything other than the best intentions, the rider's cocoon of coziness is shattered and he is compelled to respond in a manner that is completely disproportionate to the supposed crime: pure, unadulterated rage.

Take, for example, the case of the cab driver. The impatient ballsack doesn't value your safety as much as he treasures the need to get to his destination two seconds faster. Rather than waiting for you to pass, like most courteous citizens would do, he pulls out of the side road right into your path, forcing you to slam on the brakes and hope you can slow down in time. In an instant, you are wrestled from your previously calm state. Within a matter of milliseconds, the synapses in your brain fuse together, causing you to let out a stream of expletives that would make even Malcolm Tucker or Gordon Ramsay turn around to see what the fuck is going on. The cab driver then shoots off to wherever it is terrible drivers need to get to in such a hurry, leaving you to seethe and stew over the incident. The rest of the ride is then spent coming up with increasingly gruesome ways of meting out revenge, and you start to worry yourself by concocting monstrous thoughts that even Jeffrey Dahmer or Ted Bundy might think were a little on the psychopathic side.

It's not just cab drivers and cars that elicit this reaction, pedestrians do too. A boy accidentally losing control of a ball that manages to roll into your path can be scarred for life by an extreme outburst. But, remember, a kerbside dispute with a human is a lot more personal than unleashing a torrent of invective at a car. Therefore, choose your battles carefully— do you really want to risk swearing at a burly, six-foot-something body builder who's stepped into the road without looking?

In some cases, getting angry is entirely justifiable but, for the most part, it's a waste of time. Exchanges between driver and rider where they travel down the street, side by side, repeatedly screaming "You're a c***," "No, you're a c***!" at each other aren't the best idea. And, once the red mist has evaporated from in front of your eyes, it's actually rather embarrassing.

*This was written after a particularly unpleasant ride involving numerous perceived slights on my behalf, so apologies for the heightened, almost certainly unnecessary, levels of vitriol, but I thought it might help demonstrate the mindset of a cyclist scorned. Hopefully, you can tell that by the end of writing I'd managed to calm myself down!

SAFE CYCLIST

Cycling isn't a sport without risks, but then neither is golf—you might get hit by a stray ball, drive your golf cart into a ditch, get attacked by an animal, or drop dead from pure boredom. Yet this doesn't stop the participants of either sport dressing up in ridiculous clothes in preparation for a morning or afternoon of exercise.

Despite these risks, unless the golfer in question is exceptionally paranoid or insane, it's very rare to see a player on a course in a helmet. On the other hand, the bike rider is regularly seen donning some form of protective headgear while out and about. It's a sensible choice, and one that many people wouldn't argue with. After all, if your head has the displeasure of connecting with concrete, it would be a brave person who would rather they didn't have a layer of polystyrene blocking the space between skull and road. It's also rare to see a golfer equipped with a bell to ring each time he or she is about to take a shot. And yet, roads are choc-a-block with trigger-happy riders ready to sound a bell or honk a horn anytime someone dares move within a meter of the kerb edge.

When it comes to cycling, if regular trips to hospital aren't your thing, then it's simply common sense to take a few safety precautions. But that doesn't mean you have to live in constant fear of getting hurt. Yes, lights should always be used at night, but does a bike really need to be armed with an LED cannon capable of emitting a focused light beam at over 1,500 lumens? And why the need to spend hundreds on protective gear? For these guys, there's no question of sporting an old pair of shorts and a crusty old T-shirt when riding. Instead, they are decked out in protective gloves, padded trousers, and face masks to shield them from danger. It's also increasingly common to see riders with video cameras fixed to helmets, pretending they are in an episode of *Cops*, ready to capture anything untoward that comes their way. Now, while it's all well and good to take care when on a ride, heading out for a spin dressed as if you're on a peacekeeping mission to Syria is a little on the excessive side. Yet many choose to do so, and the maxim "It's better to be safe than sorry" rattles around the heads of these paranoid velocipedes like loose ball bearings in a faulty bottom bracket.

Whether or not you choose to wear protection is entirely up to you—there are sensible arguments for both and we're not here to judge. But, is there really any need to cover yourself from head-to-toe in safety gear? Cycling does have its risks, yet so does walking, driving, eating, ski-ing, and most other activities ending in –ing, yet you don't witness pedestrians crossing the road in full body armor. Surely, to be too scared to go outside, unless you're swaddled in fluorescent cloth capable of temporarily blinding anyone who shines so much as the screen of their iPhone in your direction, sucks all the joy of going for a ride. Yes, accidents can happen VERY RARELY, but preparing for carmageddon each time you set off from home is more likely to lead to stress-related illness than an actual incident with a fellow road user. So, calm down!

MOANER

Cycling is a pretty quiet sport, on the whole, with often the only audible sound being the gentle hum generated by spokes cutting through air or the metronomic tick of a chain working its way through a drive train. However, there is one sound that resonates throughout the bike-riding world— and that is the sound of moaning.

Cyclists complain about everything. From the major to the minor, no aspect of the world upon which cyclists graciously focus their attention is deemed satisfactory. Whether it's large-scale issues, such as the poor state of the roads and the lack of respect given to riders by motorists, or minor irritants like a ride potentially marred by high winds or the exorbitant cost of a puncture repair kit, there's guaranteed to be a cyclist willing to be up in arms about it. Newspaper columns are dedicated to moaning about the portrayal of cyclists in films; Twitter accounts are set up to trawl the Internet for any evidence of someone talking disparagingly about the sport; blogs are established to protest the lack of opportunities for hill climbs in certain areas; and focus groups meet up to discuss what to do about the fact that there have been several accidents in the local village because one of the hills is too steep. Hand-wringing debates on the difficulty of trying to find a place to lock your bike in town on a weekend or whether or not you should wear black socks with white shoes on a Tuesday morning seem to take up far too much time for far too many people.

Racing fans will whinge about the lack of clean riders in the sport and then when a new generation of riders comes through who look like they potentially might not actually be doping, the same fans lament that the pros are not telling the truth. Cycling campaigners wax lyrical about the lack of funding for cycling infrastructure and then when they are finally allocated some government money, it's never enough. It leaves you questioning why these people focus so much of their interest on something that clearly drives them crazy with frustration and anger.

In spite of endless tirades about the fact that you can't buy a sachet of energy gel in passion fruit flavor, the cycling community is admittedly a much better place, thanks to the hard work of many tireless (no pun intended) campaigners/moaners, and for that the riding world is eternally grateful. As a reward, perhaps the grumblers and the groaners should allow themselves a few days off the bike, as maybe they'll enjoy life a bit more?

FITNESS FREAK

Riding a bike can be fun, really great, in fact. One of the most pleasant ways to spend a day is a leisurely ride through quiet countryside, stopping for a tasty lunch in a picturesque location. Once you've finished the ride, you might even stop for a drink or two to celebrate a day of wholesome activity. But, when cycling is used as an instrument of torture in a war against physical imperfection, it becomes less of a convivial activity to while away a few hours on a sunny Saturday, and more a way to have you writhing on the floor, gasping for air like a floundering mackerel, praying you'll never have to get on a bike ever again.

You see, whenever there's something that's enjoyable, there always has to be someone to come along and suck all the fun out of it. That person is the fitness freak. The man or woman who has to push cycling to the limits of human capability. The one who doesn't see the point of a few languid laps of the local park, who would rather plan everything out instead, so that you're constantly on the verge of exhaustion, with the beats per minute of your heart never going slower than the tempo of the average drum 'n' bass track.

It used to be that you and the fitness freak were friends. You'd plan an unhurried jaunt along the river together, taking in a few waterside pubs on the way. But, just as a Russian oligarch trades in his 22-year-old wife for a younger model, you are cast aside in favor of new, fitter, faster friends who are prepared to dedicate their lives to the bike. Now, instead of stopping to eat some cake at a quaint cycle café, the only thing the fitness freak munches on is the kilometers as she heads out on another century ride, leaving you alone and upset as you face the prospect of another soul-destroying ride on your tod.

Then, there comes the judging from your former partner. The fact that you don't want to spend all your weekends with a road bike surgically attached to your butt cheeks, choosing instead to socialize with friends, enjoy a few glasses of wine, or go out for something to eat, means that you're looked upon like a larger version of Jabba the Hutt. The casting of such vehement aspersions can't be ignored, and you must take the fitness freak to task over the fact that you resent being made to feel worse than a child-killer every time you choose to take your partner out for their birthday rather than cycle for 12 hours up a mountain in a hailstorm. Otherwise, they win!

DRUG CHEAT

Ask the average person on the street today to describe pro cycling in one word and there's a good chance his or her response will be "drugs." It's an extremely sad state of affairs that many who work in or love the sport are trying to rectify, but the damage done by riders who consistently pumped their bodies full of more hormones than you'd find in a gym full of horny teenagers at a high school dance is a tough one to fix.

So, what drove these people to cheat? To carry on the one-word theme, a common answer would be "winning," and it's a hard one to argue with. When you know a great number of your rivals are skipping dessert in favor of a full blood transfusion back at the hotel room, or are stuffing themselves with cocktails of drugs that might make even Charlie Sheen think twice, it takes a stronger person than many to refuse to get involved. The clear advantages of doping meant cheating was rife and, in the 10 Tours between 1996 and 2005, you'll struggle to find a rider who featured on the podium who hasn't since been caught, admitted to, or been accused of, using performance enhancers.

The most famous of all cycling's numerous drug cheats—in fact, probably one of the biggest cheats in the history of sport, is without a doubt Lance Armstrong. Driven by an enormous will to win and an ego similar in size to the great state of Texas, where this even greater bullshitter was raised, Lance bullied, lied, blackmailed, and tricked his way to an unprecedented seven victories in the Tour de France. While he may have lacked balls in the physical sense, he certainly made up for it in metaphorical terms. His unashamedly brazen attitude meant that anyone who attempted to cross him would be disposed of, much like the vast number of needles used to juice him up into the all-conquering cycling behemoth he alluded to be.

But what can be done to solve the problem? If you have the answer, you'd better get on the phone to the cycling powers that be, as they could do with a few tips. One admittedly extreme solution that could also be pretty entertaining is to just let riders get on with it. If athletes want to spend their evenings doing jumping jacks to encourage their heart to pump treacle-like blood through the body or ingest so much EPO, the growth hormone of choice for the millennium's modern drug cheat, that it causes your urine to turn black, then let them get on with it. You have to admit, watching a group of riders fueled by more drugs than you'd find at your local doctor's surgery pushing each other to the absolute limit at speeds never before seen on a bike would be quite a sight. And the fact that their bodies teeter on the edge of their physical abilities, capable of giving up on them at any time, would only add to the spectacle and certainly make for more edge-of-your-seat viewing than the usual bike race. It would certainly give new meaning to the term "blood sport."

WANNABE PRO

There was a list posted a few years ago on the website Velominati that quickly became popular with the kind of people who frequent cycling websites… that's cyclists mainly. The list contains a series of rules which every serious rider should adhere to, including crucial edicts such as shorts must be black, socks can be any color you like, and facial hair should always be carefully maintained.

At numbers 16 and 17 of the 92-entry list are the commandments: "Respect the jersey," referring to the shirts presented to leaders and winners of races, and "Team kit is for members of the team." Despite these clear rulings, every weekend, while out on a ride, there's a good chance that you will encounter someone bathed in the amber glow of the Tour de France's yellow jersey, the conspicuous rainbow stripes of the world champion's jersey, or dressed head-to-toe in the team kit of whichever pro-cycling team is most popular at the time. But should these riders be chastized for breaking the rules or should they simply be allowed to live out their fantasies of being the next Chris Froome or Fabian Cancellera in peace, despite the fact that they are nearly old enough to be either of the riders' father?

The short answer is "no." While there's a certain endearing charm to someone over the age of 12 wanting to dress like their hero, unless you are able to get anywhere close to replicating their performances on the road, and are never overtaken by any other amateur racers, you'd best stick to brands with fewer associations with greatness, of which there are many to choose from. There's nothing more embarrassing than wearing the polka-dot jersey of the King of the Mountains, as you risk giving yourself an aneurism while struggling up a hill about as steep as the cost of a secondhand pair of cycling shorts… in other words, not very. Copying someone else's outfit has never been the cool thing to do and there's something inherently tragic about it.

If you were to take the same approach to music, and tried to resemble your idols, you'd definitely look like a bit of an idiot—perhaps going to a Lady Gaga concert with your mobile phone strapped to your head or a Kanye West gig dressed up as the world's biggest penis.

The argument is best summed up by the great Tour champion Bernard Hinault, who said, "When I see pot-bellied cyclists wearing the *maillot jaune*, it appalls me." And you don't want to mess with Bernard, as this is the guy who thought nothing of taking on numerous people who got in his way, so he'd think nothing of fighting a fat lad in a yellow jersey.

ACCIDENT-PRONE RIDER

As a cyclist, if you identify yourself with the above title, then you are a member of an unfortunate sub-section of the sport and have the sincere pity of almost every other rider out there. The Accident-prone Rider never goes out in search of an incident or an injury, but, for some reason, these things are always able to find him. Whether it's a pothole to hit at high speed, a tiny slick of oil on a wet road, or a patch of ice on a crisp winter's morning, the cursed rider will be unintentionally destined to connect with this dangerous obstacle, most likely at a high speed.

Quite why these kinds of incidents always happen to such calamitous cyclists is a mystery; it's not as if they are particularly reckless by nature. Often, they'll obey all the rules of the highway code: they'll clearly signal when making turns, never pass large vehicles on the inside, would consider listening to an iPod while riding the height of recklessness, and always cycle at sensible speeds in unfavorable conditions. However, if there's a door that's going to be suddenly flung open into the cycle path, a cab driver who is going to make an unexpected U-turn, or a pedestrian who's going to step out into the road without looking, this hapless chap will almost always find a way of being the rider who is going to play the role of the victim in this transport tragedy. Perhaps if you're a believer in the aphorism that everybody in the world is good at something, then it's quite possible that the bungling bike rider is at the forefront of the global movement for falling ass-over-tit on a regular basis.

But why then would the inept cyclist continue with a pastime that clearly doesn't gel well with the regrettable hand he's been dealt in life? A damn good question, because most people aren't gluttons for punishment—once bitten, twice shy, after all. If you are the type of person who's suffered numerous scrapes, aches, bruises, and broken bones over your cycling career, but refuse to quit, please reconsider. While we admire your commitment and perserverance, perhaps bike riding isn't the right activity for you.

Having said that, if you attempt an alternative form of transport and find yourself tripping up on the train platform or falling down the stairs on a double-decker bus, then you have our permission to give cycling another go, or maybe become a hermit instead—it's for your own good.

BMXER

Falling off a bike hurts. A lot. It's a feeling that the average rider will go out of his way to avoid doing. And, once the sensation of body connecting with concrete at a considerable speed is experienced, it's enough to make you seriously think twice about putting yourself in a similar situation. As you lie there in a heap, checking to see if all your bones are in the correct position, you do question whether riding is worth the risk.

The BMX rider never thinks like this and, instead, laughs in the face of danger—if there's no risk involved, then there's no reward. As he launches down a steep slope at around 30 mph with seven other riders, all within touching distance, any concerns for personal safety are thrown out of the window because it's time to get extreme. When the group hits jumps that launch them over 5ft into the air, crashes aren't just a small possibility, they're almost a foregone conclusion. These accidents often take out at least half the field, sometimes considerably more. You see, with BMX racing, abbreviated from bicycle motocross, anything can, and often does, happen.

So, what inspires a rider to embrace his inner masochist and ignore the ever-present risk of cuts, bruises, and broken bones? The answer: he's an idiot, at least when it comes to self-preservation. Yet it can't be denied that the thrill of hitting a corner so fast that your one solitary brake can't slow you down, forcing you to skid into the turn, overcook it, go flying off the track, and scrape off most of the skin on your left leg and elbow is one that's hard to resist. Or maybe not. These risks only make up one part of BMXing: track riding. On the other side of the sport you have the freestyle guys, who eschew racing in favor of solo jaunts on the streets, along trails, or in specially designed parks. These adrenaline junkies—who, unlike their track-racing brethren, have a strange allergic reaction to safety clothing, instead choosing the somewhat limited protection offered by millimeter-thin layers of human skin—enjoy nothing more than repeatedly throwing themselves down massive flights of stairs until they manage to land ludicrously named tricks such as the magic carpet or can can. Or, maybe, they'll head to the half pipe and continue in their questionable quest to fracture a wrist or a pelvis by spinning round 720 degrees and landing backward. It's very impressive to see someone achieve such a feat of athleticism and, as the watching crowds cheer a successful attempt, the rider flashes a toothless grin (they lost some front incisors following an aborted superman seat grab) of satisfaction that makes all the risks worthwhile.

MOUNTAIN BIKER

My ankle, my collarbone twice, my wrist, and my thumb, and more cuts, scrapes, and bruises than I'd like to remember. So, yeah, I guess you could say there's an element of danger, but without the risks, you don't get the rewards. You see, as far as I'm concerned, there's nothing more thrilling than throwing yourself down a steep track on the side of a mountain or through a forest. You know it's not the safest thing to do, but you stick that to the back of your mind and try to ignore it. Much as I do when I have the misfortune of coming across the words Miley and Cyrus. You see, with a bit of practice and skill, you reduce your chances of falling off by at least two percent. I like those odds!

The feelings I get when I huck* a massive gap, land a huge drop perfectly, flow a trail like a boss, or beat my downhill personal best time are pretty incredible. I always try to take a moment to remember how I felt at the time. That way, when I'm lying in a hospital bed having blown out my collarbone again, I can go to my happy place and try to remind myself why I got myself in this mess once more. But, you know what, it's easy to keep coming back to the sport, because the people you come across while out on a ride, waiting for a cable car, in the bike shop, or in the emergency room are super-chilled and friendly. So, when you stack it badly, there's always a smiling face there ready to ring an ambulance for you, attempt to click a dislocated bone back into its socket, or help you find the various pieces of shattered bike that have scattered around the mountain.

*Ed—nope, me neither

All these little things help to restore your faith in humanity, so God bless all my fellow mountain bikers out there. People could learn a lot from these guys. If we all rode trails and did downhill together, the world would be a much nicer place. You could argue that it might not be a safer place from a personal injury sense, but the positives of regularly getting extreme far outweigh the negatives. Killjoys might also say that the hospitals would be a lot busier dealing with injured bikers, that we'd all be a bit poorer as we'd have to keep on shelling out to get our bikes fixed, or that we wouldn't be able to do stuff that easily because of the occasional broken bone. All I can reply to that is killjoys suck! At the end of the day, these really are small sacrifices to make because mountain biking is awesome.

TANDEM COUPLE

The couple that rides together, stays together. Or, at least that's what the tandem bike riders like to think as they ride past yet another person completely baffled by why anyone would want to spend their free time staring at their riding partner's backside.

There's something a little sinister about the co-dependent nature of tandem users that's rather unsettling. The way they go everywhere in pairs confuses anyone who enjoys the feeling of independence that cycling can give you. They are like a bike riding version of the scary twins from *The Shining*, drunk girls out on a Friday night who are incapable of going to the bathroom by themselves, or the most horrendous pairing of all time: Jedward.

And then you start to question why it is that these couples can't ride their own bikes. Where does the need to be attached to the same frame as someone else come from? Is the desire to pedal everywhere in unison linked to a subconscious wish to feel wanted, is it caused by an innate need to never be alone, or is it fueled by an extrovert personality that likes to stand out from the crowd? And how do the tandem riders choose who gets to go at the front and who's stuck at the rear? The front is clearly the better option, as you get to steer and take in the view, while the person at the back is, instead, forced to monitor the progress of the ever-expanding sweat patch developing on the back of the lead rider's shirt.

Is one person the dominant one, the trouser-wearing captain of the bike, leading the other along a road they'd otherwise be incapable of tackling? Or, are they simply the kind of partnership that feels the need to do everything together— the sort of pairing who fill their Instagram feeds with constant pictures of their #BFF or the #wifey/hubby? Perhaps the desire to feel their bodies united together by steel frame and chain inspires them. Whatever the answers, as the riders' legs spin round and round in unison, it's a bit like watching the bike world's version of synchronized swimming, complete with ridiculous headgear and creepy perma-smiles.

Admittedly, given half the chance, most people with even a passing interest in cycling would love to have a go on a tandem, but, after the novelty of sharing a frame quickly wears off, the vast majority will be very happy to get back to their own bikes. The average tandem rider is probably a lovely person, but then so is the woman who lives in a home filled with 50 cats or the man who collects My Little Pony dolls well into middle age. These behaviors could easily be dismissed as quirky or eccentric, or could there be something rather more foreboding lurking beneath the layers of matching lycra?

THE WEIRD & WONDERFUL

Apart from the odd tweak, the shape of the commercial bike frame has changed very little over the last 100 years or so. It's a testament to this design classic that the shape has endured for over a century. And yet, the cycling world has never been short of people willing to create their own unique takes on the traditional blueprint.

From bikes with frames welded on top of frames and rides with coffee machines attached to the front to the classic penny farthing, with its ridiculously unbalanced wheel set, cyclists have never been shy of trying new ideas. Always ready with a well-stocked toolkit and blow torch, they will experiment with endless configurations attempting to discover new ways to push forward the cycling experience. And not all these enterprises are crackpot schemes; some are highly effective. Take the recumbent bike where the rider sits on a seat inches from the ground with the pedals stretched out in front of the rear wheel. By keeping low to the ground, the aerodynamic benefits are hard to argue with and riders achieve speeds that are quicker than the more traditional road bike is capable of. Then, there's Old Faithful, the homemade bike designed by Graeme Obree that allowed him to adopt the more aerodynamic, arms-out-in-front position, so helping him to break the world hour record.

On the other side of the coin are countless bizarre creations, such as the bike with a shopping trolley attached to the front instead of a wheel or the bike that acts as a moving bar, where 10 or more riders can enjoy a beer and a chat as they pedal. Whatever the inspiration for the inventors, you've got to hand it to them for being sufficiently off the wall to carry out their visions and not give a shit what other people think, because, let's face it, you need to be quite thick-skinned if you're in the business of coming up with outlandish inventions. Even the biggest, buffest, coolest, slickest, most handsome cycling fanatic is going to struggle to look anything other than a bit of a tit when riding a wooden bike with a treadmill attached to it or one that's made from a toilet.

It's not just the shape of the bike that people are compelled to tweak, it's also how they use it. You've got the more obvious examples, such as the mountain bike where people decided to take traditional bikes off road, but have you ever witnessed the absolutely bonkers sport of artistic cycling? Here, a rider (or riders as they often appear in pairs or as a team) mimics a dance or gymnastics routine by performing a series of acrobatic maneuvers—such as no-handed wheelies or riding the bike while standing on the handlebars—to a musical soundtrack. A quick search on YouTube will soon enlighten you to the frankly insane, yet strangely compelling, world of bike dancing.

BIKE NERD

Geeks—every sport has them, and cycling's no different. In bedrooms and bike shops, gear freaks are working themselves into a frenzy over the latest technological developments. Evenings are spent on bike forums partaking in debates about the benefits of osymetric rings in limiting the dead spot of a pedal cycle or comparing the firmware and user functionality of different brands of power meter. Basically, if there's any element of a bike that has been improved or feat of engineering that can be deconstructed, they need to know about it.

Nerds lust after the equipment used by the pros and dream of a time when the cycling app they are developing becomes a hit so that they can fund their addiction to carbon fiber and other lightweight materials. They pour over any press release from a bike manufacturer to check what the latest developments are and count down the days to annual trade shows such as Eurobike in Germany or Interbike in the United States. These events are a dream-come-true for bike-porn addicts, as it's here that they get to experience first-hand the cutting edge technologies that bike manufacturers have been developing. Once through the doors, obsessives can't contain their excitement, as they struggle to decide which company to visit first. They really want to see in the flesh the bike ridden by this year's Tour winner and the new suspension fork featuring tunable low-speed compression. But they are torn, as they also heard rumors of a pair of bib shorts with hitherto unheard-of levels of padding that they are desperate to touch—after all, chamois don't squeeze themselves.

The cameras on smart phones are barely able to focus, as users shake with excitement at the unveiling of a new shoe that allows wearers to tighten the buckle in 2- rather than 3-millimeter increments. First-aiders have to be called to stands to revive several attendees after they faint at the news that the latest power units for electronic transmission systems could not only be mounted internally within the frame tubing but had also lost around 1oz (30g) in weight. And, if you have any clue what that means, you really should get out more.

The funny thing is, although they know nearly all there is to know about bike technologies and performance, they'll never get to actually use the equipment they lust after. Unless they have high-flying jobs in banking, run a successful business, are part of a pro-cycling team, or are lucky enough to win the lottery, the price tags attached to equipment that'll shave off a few grams from the weight of your bike, or ensure your gear changes are a fraction of a second quicker, are so high that you'd have to sell your comic collection to invest in them. So, until that golden ticket is purchased, nerds can only fantasize about what it's like to ride on a cutting-edge bike.

$5,000.00

FORUM USER

John couldn't wait to get home. It'd been a tough day of long meetings and it wasn't until 8pm that he'd finally left the office. Usually, a day like this would put him in a foul mood and all he'd want to do when he got in was head straight for bed. But something wonderful had happened on his lunch break that had made the past 12 hours bearable.

While queuing for a burrito, John saw a cyclist in the distance, a flash of neon on the horizon. "Hello," John said to himself, "That's not... surely... it is!' As the rider came closer, John could clearly make out a track frame with BMX handlebars and a bright green saddle. To make matters even worse, the rider had put deep rims on the bike. Not only that, the rims were bright pink! "What year does this chump think it is, 2009?"

To John's delight, the rider pulled up a few feet away, locked his bike, and went into a café. The opportunity was too good to miss and John hastily took some snaps of the bike. "Just wait until the boys on the forum see this," he grinned. And it was these images that kept John going for the rest of the day at work—knowing that he had on his camera pictures that were going to be the talk of the *Track Or Single Speed Enthusiasts and Riders* website.

TOSSER was one of the biggest bike forums on the web, where users got together to discuss all things bike-related—from the "sickest" NJS frames from Tokyo to the latest Internet memes. John had signed up to TOSSER a year ago and had slowly worked his way from newbie status to forum regular. He'd survived the initial bouts of banter aimed at him by the other forum members, kept his head down, and slowly built up his post count with a series of inoffensive missives about bike parts. He'd commented enthusiastically on more established members' posts, gently massaging their egos until they started to take notice of him.

Soon John was invited to attend one of the regular forum meet-ups and he spent the entire day before preparing his bike, making sure his Chris King headset was perfectly polished and Brooks saddle was scuff-free. His ride was well received, he identified the main faces on the forum, and laughed at all their jokes. He also slated a few kids who had put mountain bike pedals on a road bike, which went down very well with the other attendees. After John left, he felt certain that a place in the forum's inner circle was finally within his grasp. All he needed to achieve this goal was make one exceptional post to prove his

skills in the piss-taking department, and he was in. And now, armed with the pictures of this hideous bike, he had the material needed to boost his forum rep to the next level.

John walked through the front door, said a quick hello to his parents, and then ran up the stairs to upload the photos to the *When Bikes Go Bad* thread. A few seconds later and the pics were up, along with the caption: "What is this afterbirth of a bike about? #Clueless #nOOb #Megalolz"

John sat for five minutes waiting for his first reply, certain that this would have the forum bods LOL'ing out. Ten minutes later and nobody had responded. Perhaps there was a problem with the Internet connection, so John clicked refresh just to make sure. The page updated without a hitch, but no comments appeared. This was very odd, it's not like other forum members would be out riding bikes; it was much more fun to sit in front of a laptop and talk about them. Confused, he decided to try and forget about it and went to bed.

Several hours later, John was woken suddenly by a chime from his laptop. He jumped out of bed and rushed to the screen. He felt exhilarated—his time had come, he was now a recognized face on the forum. As his eyes adjusted to the brightness of the screen, he saw a message from Fixuplooksharp, one of the founding members of the forum. In the subject line was the word BANNED. John was confused: what did this mean? He read on…

Dear Beersandgears (aka John),

As you are aware, members are not allowed to comment negatively on the bikes of other forum users. We are part of a community dedicated to pointing out flaws with the bikes of non-members in the hope that we influence and change people's attitudes, shaping them to become more like our own. As a result, it serves no purpose to attack the bikes of fellow

Forum User

*members, as they have exceptional taste. In this case, the bike
you criticized is my own; it is amazing, and you are wrong. Your
negativity is not welcome in this community and your account
has been terminated.*

John was devastated. He realized what had happened. While
he'd been stuck in a meeting, he hadn't been able to check the
latest posts and see that tastes had changed. That was the way
it was in the world of the bike forum—fashions were fickle and
could change in an instant. If you didn't keep up, you were out.
He slumped back in the chair and let out a deep sigh. "Back to
square one," he mused, before sitting up and starting to type
on the computer. "Now, where am I going to be able to get
some BMX bars and pink rims?"

SUPER FAN

Every year, my boss knows I'm taking a week off in spring and then a longer three-week binge— I mean trip—in the summer. Any cycling fan knows why—come late March/early April, it's Spring Classics season, then over the summer I've got the choice of three grand tours: the Giro, the Tour de France, or La Vuelta. I change it up each year, so that I don't get bored of the local booze. Only joking—I'll drink anything—but it is nice to compare the bars and Irish pubs of Italy, Spain, and France. Plus, there's the non-stop cycling action to look forward to. Wahey!

The Belgian cycling fans are absolutely ace, great banter. They love the sport and the beers almost as much as me. Even in some of the crappiest weather, there'll be a few crazy guys mad enough to join me in strawpedoeing six bottles of super-strength Trappist beer, then stripping down to our boxers to cheer on local heroes like Tom Boonen or Philippe Gilbert. The year Phil cleaned up at all three of the Ardennes Classics, I don't think I've ever drunk so much in my life. It was wild. I woke up on the Monday morning by the side of La Redoute, with only one shoe, no jeans, a massive Flanders flag, and a hangover as epic as Phil's win. I'd also managed to lose my wallet and getting to the airport for my flight home was a nightmare. I made it in the end but, at the departure gate, I was in a terrible state, vomming left, right, and center. I didn't know what was going on. They nearly didn't let me on. Luckily, the old gray matter kicked in long enough for me to mutter something about a bad batch of moules frites and they relented.

I love the Spring Classics because the riders are hardcore tough guys. I model my drinking on them—go big or go home—but the weather is always shocking. That's why the grand tours are the ones I really look forward to, as more often than not the sun is out and the booze is free-flowing. First up is the Giro d'Italia. It's perhaps not as famous internationally as the Tour de France, but it's got its own ultra-patriotic atmosphere that's

perfect for anyone looking to party. The Italians, or the Tifosi, as us cycling heads call them, know their sport inside out, which means at the roadside there's so much history and passion (and drinking)—quality! Former winners are treated like gods over there, particularly Coppi, Bartali, Gimondi, Pantani, Nibali, and anyone else with a name ending in –i who's won it. You only have to mention those names at a bar and you've made a friend for the day to share a bottle (or 10!) of the local vino. Perfect.

The mountain stages are the best, as that's where you get the true cycle nutters. Every Tour has their classics, like the Stelvio Pass in the Italian Alps or Mont Ventoux in France. Then there's newer ones such as the mental Bola del Mundo near Madrid. But, if you're like me, and love a rave, Dutch Corner on the climb to Alpe D'Huez has got to be up there with Spring Break, St. Patrick's Day, or Oktoberfest, as the ultimate smash-up destination. Just picture the scene: the biggest bike race in the world, thousands of Dutch Bantersaurs ready to create carnage, the best Eurodance tunes banging out from the speakers, a sea of Orange as far as the eye can see, and an endless supply of Heineken. When a Dutch rider comes round the corner, everyone loses their shit, and all the top boys in their keerrazzzeee outifts chase after him. And, of course, I'm there at the front, beer in one hand, flare in the other. Hup Holland!

I do enjoy mixing it up with the boys from the Basque Country and the other Spanish lunatics during the Vuelta. They know how to party and go absolutely bonkers when any orange Euskatel (RIP) rider launches a carrot attack. I tell you what, it's *muy caliente* in that part of the world in August and early September, but it's nothing that a few chilled lad juices won't fix. The scenery on some of the stages is amazing… the girls are well tasty! The mountains aren't too bad either—the lakes of Covadonga (ha, I said dong!) are great for a bit of skinny dipping with the señoritas once the peleton's gone past. #Megaladz!

Super Fan

APOLOGIST

I take it I'm not the only one who's noticed how motorists all hate cyclists, wish we were banned from the roads, want to kill us, etc. Just to gauge some opinion, I've personally never really noticed much hatred from motorists. And, frankly, I'm pretty disgusted. Disgusted by what other cyclists are doing to perpetrate this terrible reputation we have. It's enough to make me want to quit riding.

I find cab and van drivers to be some of the most considerate, conscientious road users out there. How could they not be, given the amount of time they spend on the roads? And other road users I don't even notice 99 percent of the time. When a car did pull out and hit me, the driver immediately tried to help, said it was an accident, he didn't see me, etc. Fair enough. I apologized to him for the inconvenience I'd caused to his journey and for the bump I'd made in his bonnet. Once we'd managed to stem the bleeding from my nose, I went to the ATM and gave him the money to get the bonnet repaired. We were firm friends after that and, hopefully, I did something to encourage rider-driver relations. I believe everyone should just get on and I'm not afraid to be the bigger man and accept someone made a mistake. We can all be a bit silly sometimes.

There was another incident when I hit the side of a cab. It was a bit of a shock, but I hold my hands up again—it was my fault. The driver was on the phone, decided to do a U-turn without signaling and came across me, but really I should have been able to anticipate his move. Some cyclists came and accused the driver of being reckless and offered to be witnesses for me, but I sent them packing. I want nothing to do with this gang mentality, this us-versus-them culture of blame, thank you very much. It all worked out in the end, though, as the motorist was a nice guy. He drove both me and my broken bike to the hospital, and then only charged me for half the fare.

The main people I have an issue with are cyclists. I regularly feel the need to apologize for their behavior. Every morning, in rush hour, when we're all trying to get to work, 50 percent of cyclists, thinking they are somehow more important than other road users, don't stick as close to the curb as they could and sometimes stray into the road. It's simple common sense that you don't want to make the drivers of bigger vehicles angry; you need to keep out of the way at all times. Cycling guys need to know their place. They're slower than other traffic, so move it!

I tell you who else grinds my gears: riders that remonstrate with drivers who sound their horns loudly to tell cyclists to get out the way. The motorist will often say something about riders not paying road tax and the rider will make up some nonsense that there is no such thing as road tax. It is so annoying that, occasionally, I've been known to shout, "You ignorant idiot, stop lying!" because I feel like drivers should know we're not all like that. I often question whether this is betraying my cycling brethren but, you know what, they deserve to be called out. The car is king and that isn't going to change any time soon.

INDEX

ACKNOWLEDGMENTS

Thanks to Paul Parker for his excellent illustrations, Caroline West for her
editing skills, and to all the people at Dog 'n' Bone. Thanks to all BBC/SLCC
riders for waiting for me at the top of hills. Thank you to my dad for rocking
denim hot pants whenever he rode and my mum for supporting every fad.

Finally, thanks to Chloe—one day I promise to find somewhere to store my
bike other than the hallway.